THE INCARNATE WORD

The Incarnate Word

Perspectives on Jesus in the Fourth Gospel

Marianne Meye Thompson

HENDRICKSON
PUBLISHERS
PEABODY, MASSACHUSETTS 01961-3473

COPYRIGHT © 1988 HENDRICKSON PUBLISHERS, INC.

Hendrickson Publishers, Inc.
P. O. Box 3473
Peabody, MA 01961-3473

ISBN 1-56563-025-4

This work was originally titled *The Humanity of Jesus in the Fourth Gospel* and was published in 1988 by Fortress Press.

CONTENTS

PREFACE

Not so very long ago, I was tempted to begin this preface by citing Huck Finn's words that "if I'd 'a' knowed what a trouble it was to make a book I wouldn't 'a' tackled it." But as the task now draws to its close, it seems far less trouble, especially as I pause to thank those who helped me to tackle it. Indeed it is no trouble, but a pleasure, to express my gratitude to those who in one way or another were instrumental in bringing this manuscript to birth.

I would like first to acknowledge the debt I owe my parents for their support, a support which has remained constant through the years, beyond the completion of my doctoral studies. The years of schooling have been many, and my parents have helped make them pleasant, rewarding, and possible. Furthermore, it is through their guidance and example that the subject matter of the present book is not merely a topic of academic interest but a reality of life and faith. To them I dedicate this book with respect, appreciation, and love.

I have had other important teachers along the way, but here I should like to single out two who sparked my interest in the Gospel of John: Gordon Fee, now of Regent College, and the late Glenn Barker, my friend and professor at Fuller Theological Seminary. To both I owe thanks for inspiring teaching, faithful scholarship, and encouragement to pursue a path which, then as now, is not often taken by women.

Foremost among the teachers whose labors are related to this work, however, is Professor D. Moody Smith of Duke University. Those who have had the privilege to work with him respect his erudition and able supervision, tendered in a spirit of cordiality and patience. Those who know his work in the Gospel of John respect his circumspect judgment and careful scholarship. I would like to thank him for his diligent shepherding of the dissertation which lies behind this manuscript, as well as for his continuing friendship and help. He is a happy exception to Paul's words that "not many are wise"!

Some measure of thanks is also due to my daughter, Allison Joy, who delayed her entrance into the world just long enough to allow me to get this manuscript to the publisher. But above all, I would like to express my gratitude to my husband John who has shared with me the years of graduate school not only as an onlooker, but as a colleague. Many times he has found the right word or thought when I could not. His theological and historical insights have made the enterprise always more lively and stimulating, and his sacrifice of time made it possible for me to reach more than one deadline. In the midst of pursuing his own studies, he has steadfastly been my *syzygos kai synergos gnesios*.

MARIANNE MEYE THOMPSON

Fuller Theological Seminary
Pasadena, California

INTRODUCTION

THE PROBLEM OF JESUS' HUMANITY IN THE FOURTH GOSPEL

And the Word became flesh and dwelt among us, full of grace and truth; we have beheld his glory, glory as of the only Son from the Father. (John 1:14)

THE PROBLEM IN RECENT DISCUSSION

Bultmann and Käsemann in Debate

One of the most influential, albeit highly controversial, studies of the Fourth Gospel in recent decades is Ernst Käsemann's, *The Testament of Jesus*.[1] Although the book's subtitle, "A Study of the Gospel of John in Light of Chapter 17," suggests an exegetical analysis of that chapter, this is no plodding commentary. Rather, the study offers a provocative and sometimes irritating sketch of Johannine theology. It is irritating not simply because one may disagree with it and challenge its method and the conclusions, but also because it often finds a tender spot and rubs mercilessly against it. In this instance that tender spot is the traditional portrayal of Johannine Christology.

In his first chapter, "The Glory of Christ," Käsemann develops the thesis that the Johannine Christology ought to be called "naively docetic." Contrary to scholarly and popular opinion, it is scarcely adequate to give rise to the dogmatic formulations of the fourth and fifth centuries which characterized Jesus as "true man" (*vere*

1

homo/alēthos anthrōpos). In John, Jesus' divine glory so overshadows his humanity that the traditional exposition of John 1:14 as
the hallmark of the Gospel's incarnational theology must be
abandoned.

Käsemann's explication cuts against the grain of much interpretation of the Gospel as the champion of the incarnation of the Word.
Traditionally, John 1:14 is understood to reveal the mystery of the
person of Jesus—he is the Word made flesh—and perhaps even to
emphasize his humanity against encroaching Docetism, particularly
as the portrait of it emerges in 1 John. In rejecting this interpretation, Käsemann's study, although it does not say so, essentially
constitutes a challenge not only to Johannine studies, but specifically to the view of his teacher, Rudolf Bultmann. Certainly Bultmann is no proponent of either John's "orthodoxy" or the ac-
ceptability of the evangelist's viewpoints to the church at large. Yet
his interpretation of 1:14 yields a somewhat orthodox interpretation of the humanity of Jesus in the Fourth Gospel. Bultmann var-
iously writes that the theme of the Gospel is the "Word made flesh,"
the Revealer is "nothing but a man," and Jesus is the Revealer in
his "sheer humanity."[2] Needless to say, Käsemann's interpretation
of the Johannine Christology stands diametrically opposed to Bultmann's, for Bultmann argues that in John one confronts the paradox of revelation present in hiddenness. Precisely because revelation is hidden, one can focus only on the undeniably real flesh,
the "sheer humanity" of the Revealer, Jesus, in order to see that
revelation.

Whereas Bultmann takes as the theme of John's Gospel "the
Word became flesh" (1:14a), Käsemann locates the substance of
the Gospel's witness in the subsequent confession, "and we beheld
his glory" (1:14b). Whereas Bultmann stresses the sheer humanity
of the Revealer, Käsemann stresses the Revealer's glory—that is,
his divinity—supremely attested in the church's confession of the
Word as God (1:14; 20:28).[3] On the one hand, then, Bultmann
speaks of seeing the divine glory in the man Jesus; the presence of
God's glory in no way effaces Jesus' very real humanity. On the
other hand, Käsemann concludes that the Johannine Christology

of glory verges on the brink of Docetism and the denial of Jesus' true humanity.[4]

Criticisms of Käsemann's Approach

Käsemann's study constitutes a thoroughgoing challenge to Bultmann's delineation of the fundamental contours of Johannine theology, particularly at the points of Christology and John's relationship to Gnosticism. But many scholars, including fellow students of Bultmann's, remained unconvinced by Käsemann's efforts to reshape so drastically the interpretation of the Gospel.[5] If Bultmann's readers and students were not persuaded, neither have Käsemann's critics been content to let him have the final say. Indeed, more than one scholar has sought to steer a safer course between the Scylla and Charybdis of these opposing interpretations of the Gospel and its Christology.[6]

The debate between Bultmann and Käsemann threw into sharp relief the question of the Johannine depiction of the Christ. It turned in part on exegesis, and one may legitimately question the exegesis of various passages of the Gospel offered by Käsemann and Bultmann. Furthermore, one may also challenge their different methods in approaching the Gospel. Bultmann's theories of the sources, of the displacements and rearrangements behind the present Gospel, and of their implications for interpreting the biblical text, have been adequately criticized and discussed.[7] My particular concern is Käsemann's approach to the Gospel, which has also been challenged, especially in his use of the "testament of Jesus" in chapter 17 as the starting point for his discussion.[8] By beginning with chapter 17, Käsemann focuses on what is peculiar or unique to John. He thereby overlooks aspects of the portrait of Jesus which are also characteristic of the Gospel and therefore must equally be taken into account. Many of those things which are characteristic of John's description of Jesus may be related specifically to the consideration of Jesus' humanity. For example, his parents (2:1–11; 6:42; 19:25–27) and brothers (6:42; 2:12; 7:3, 10) are mentioned more than once; at the well in Samaria he is weary (4:6) and asks for a drink (4:7); he has friends (11:1–3), and is moved at the death of one of them (11:33, 35); and his life ends in death. With the exception of

Jesus' death, these other events and references appear in material or settings which have no obvious counterparts in the Synoptic tradition and which must therefore be called characteristic of the Fourth Gospel. Yet these same texts depict Jesus in terms which would be quite at home in any of the Synoptic Gospels.[9]

On the other hand, in comparison with the Synoptic Gospels it is undeniable that chapter 17 stands out as peculiar to John. But by interpreting the entire Gospel from its perspective without taking into account other features of John's portrayal, Käsemann's account has skewed the resulting Christology. As Stephen Smalley writes, "Käsemann's version of John's christology is decidedly unbalanced. While elements in the Johannine portrait of Jesus are capable of a docetic interpretation *if taken by themselves*, the total effect can scarcely be regarded as one of 'divinity without humanity.' "[10]

Beyond the objections which one may raise against Käsemann's exegetical conclusions and method, one may lodge a protest against his presuppositions in approaching the Gospel. Particularly problematic is his application to the Gospel of a definition of humanity which is extraneous to the Gospel itself. On Käsemann's terms, "naively docetic" is a phrase which summarizes John's unconvincing portrayal of Jesus as a human being. As Käsemann readily acknowledges, his assessment of the Gospel in these terms is not original. He particularly lauds the writings of F. C. Baur, William Wrede, G. P. Wetter, and Emanuel Hirsch, whom he deems to have properly interpreted and presented John's Christology as a Christology of glory.[11]

Among their shared emphases are: (1) an interpretation of the incarnation which rejects the view that Jesus became fully, truly human (Baur); (2) a denial that Jesus' human traits or characteristics, taken together, yield a believable picture of a human being (Wrede, Wetter, Hirsch); and (3) a characterization of the Johannine Christology as "docetic" (Baur) or as "God walking on the earth" (Wrede, Wetter). Implicit in such modern critical judgments is a subjective definition of "humanity" against which John's portrait of Jesus has been measured and found wanting.

According to Käsemann, there are three components crucial to "humanity" which are lacking in John's Jesus.

1. Jesus lacks the desirable traits of compassion, mercy, kindness, and so on, which would make him truly sympathetic and thereby presumably "truly human"—especially in twentieth-century eyes. While both Bultmann and Käsemann use the term "human" to denote that which contrasts to the divine, Käsemann subtly shifts the emphasis by enlarging the definition of "human" to include the component of "acting humanely," that is, possessing those traits he sees as desirable in a human being. Thus when he objects that John's portrait of Jesus is not that of a "true man," he comments specifically on Jesus' demeanor: "He dissociates himself from the Jews, as if they were not his own people and he meets his mother as the one who is her Lord. He permits Lazarus to lie in the grave for four days in order that the miracle of his resurrection may be more impressive."[12]

2. Käsemann contends that in the Fourth Gospel Jesus is never truly exposed to the suffering and pain of this world, nor is he subject to the vicissitudes of existence on earth.

3. Käsemann seems to say that for one to be truly human one may not manifest any traits except those common to all human beings. A Jesus who is "always on the side of God" shows no solidarity with humanity.

For Käsemann, then, John 1:14 cannot be the hallmark of John's incarnational Christology because the way in which Jesus is depicted in the rest of the Gospel disallows it. Jesus is not portrayed as a real, suffering, finite human being. Instead, the evangelist emphasizes Jesus' glory—his divinity—to the extent that he can be called "God on earth." Here there is no paradox of the divine Word assuming human flesh, for there is no real humiliation or oneness with humanity, and thus no real humanity.

In short, while Käsemann purports to address the question "Does John portray a fully human Jesus?" he rather answers the question "Does John portray a fully sympathetic Jesus?" Instead of asking whether the evangelist believes in a fully human Jesus, Käsemann asks whether we find the portrait of Jesus as a human being fully believable. "Do [features of lowliness] characterize John's Christology in such a manner that through them the 'true man' of later incarnational theology becomes believable?"[13]

It is precisely the question of whether the Johannine portrait of Christ is a convincing portrait of a human being—a key question for Käsemann and his predecessors—which has not proved fruitful for further study. Wayne Meeks aptly sums up the objection when he responds to Käsemann's contention that "judged by the modern concept of reality, our Gospel is more fantastic than any other writing of the New Testament."[14] Meeks writes:

> Is that the actual issue? Even the Chalcedonian Christology is pretty fantastic "judged by the modern concept of reality," but it is not thereby *docetic*. Käsemann succeeds in making us face up to the strangeness of the Johannine Christology, and that is a significant accomplishment. But a more precise definition of that strangeness is called for.[15]

In short, how "fantastic" or unconvincing we find John's picture of the human Jesus is not the issue; and scholars writing in the wake of Käsemann's *The Testament of Jesus* have not followed his lead at this point.

AN ALTERNATIVE APPROACH
TO THE QUESTION

Clearly, then, disagreement with Käsemann has arisen at several points. In its basic structure and approach the present study takes issue with Käsemann's (1) presuppositions, (2) exegetical conclusions, and (3) method. I disagree with Käsemann's exegesis that the Gospel represents a "naively docetic" view of Jesus because I reject the anachronistic way in which he has framed the question. Käsemann assesses the Gospel as docetic in part because of his method and in part because of his presuppositions: he focuses exclusively on chapter 17, thereby overlooking data in other chapters that are also pertinent to the issue of Jesus' humanity in John; and he approaches the Gospel with a rigid definition of humanity. In order to attempt to circumvent these same problems, I will proceed on the following assumptions relating to (1) presuppositions and the definition of humanity, (2) the issues which will be discussed exegetically, and (3) the general approach or method adopted in pursuing that exegesis.

The Definition of Humanity

In order to investigate Jesus' humanity according to the Fourth Gospel, one must allow the Gospel to define "humanity"—that, of course, is the exegete's ideal. Obviously John nowhere gives an abstract definition of "humanity," nor does he address how and in what way the term is applicable to Jesus. Neither can the exegete come to the Gospel without some idea already in mind of what it is appropriate to investigate in discussing "humanity." How can we raise what is almost certainly more a twentieth- than a first-century question without completely predetermining the results? There is no way to approach the Gospel and raise the question of Jesus' humanity with our minds unprejudiced; the circularity of the interpretative process is inescapable.

But if, as I have argued, Käsemann's definition of humanity is too rigid, are there categories for constructing a definition that does not force John's portrait of Jesus onto a procrustean bed? I think that better categories may be found—"softer" categories, so to speak—which allow the text to speak more on its own terms. To employ such categories involves approaching the Gospel with a notion of the meaning of "human" that is at least open-ended and subject to correction, asking how and on what terms the evangelist describes Jesus and his activity in this world.

What is it, then, about the life and activity of "human beings in this world" that can be called characteristic and thereby might provide more appropriate categories or avenues of inquiry into the Gospel? At the very least, to be human means to be differentiated from animals on the one hand and God on the other; accordingly, certain elements—birth, family, life activities, death—constitute the outline of what we expect to be told about any human being. Obviously these bare facts cannot simply be added up to "prove" that someone is fully human. But these essential "moments" of a person's life constitute categories by which the totality of that life can be investigated. In the language and thought of the Fourth Gospel, these categories correspond to Jesus' human origins and flesh, which together describe his relationship to other human beings and the realities of this material world; his "signs," which constitute the focal point of his activity in this world; and the passion narrative, where the end of his life is related. These categories have emerged repeatedly in recent Johannine studies as crucial issues for interpreting the Gospel.

Jesus' Origins

Under the heading of Jesus' origins, the problem to be discussed is the relationship of Jesus' human origins to his heavenly ones. Granted, the Fourth Gospel asserts that Jesus has come "from above," from God; but it also affirms his human origins and parentage (1:46; 4:43–45; 7:25–52; 12:34). The problem is the relationship of these two realities. Does the Gospel, as some have argued, give evidence of a dualism that denies the significance of all earthly realities, including Jesus' earthly origins, and thereby contributes to the characterization of Jesus as alien to and separated from this world?[16] Or does the Gospel shatter that dualism by insisting upon the importance of Jesus' this-worldly existence and origins?[17]

The Incarnation in John

A second and closely related aspect of the problem centers on the Johannine view of the incarnation, particularly as expressed in 1:14. As noted, Bultmann and Käsemann take different components of this verse as decisive for interpreting the Gospel's theme. Since the publication of *The Testament of Jesus*, interest in the prologue and 1:14 has scarcely abated. Recent studies, however, have not approached its interpretation by asking Käsemann's question; namely, is the portrait of Jesus in the Gospel adequate to allow us to argue that 1:14 asserts a "genuine incarnation"? They have not focused so much on Jesus' earthly life—that is, on his behavior and actions—as defining the meaning of the incarnation. Rather, they have focused on the evangelist's viewpoint toward "this-worldly" realities as embodied in his use of the term *sarx* (flesh), both in 1:14 and in other passages in the Gospel. This trend offers a fruitful approach both to the interpretation of 1:14 and to John's view of the humanity of Jesus.

Jesus' Signs

According to recent scholarship, the evangelist's viewpoint toward "this-worldly" realities finds particular expression not only in his attitude toward flesh but also in his view of signs, which constitute an essential ingredient of Jesus' activity in the world.[18] Moreover, there is an increasing insistence that flesh (*sarx*) and signs (*sēmeia*) must be seen together as expressing the Fourth Gospel's view of material realities, particularly as they are the occasion for faith in Jesus. Is the material reality itself, the sign which Jesus does, important in understanding that sign and, ultimately, who Jesus is? Or is the sign itself irrelevant, or perhaps merely a symbol of a greater spiritual reality? By endeavoring to uncover the Johannine perception of the significance of signs for faith, one gains a further insight into John's view of material realities. When the Johannine view of signs is correlated with John's view of Jesus' origins, incarnation and flesh, one obtains an understanding of John's view of Jesus' existence in this world. Thereby one avoids the cul-de-sac into which the question of whether or not the Johannine view of Jesus' humanity is convincing ultimately leads.

The Death of Jesus

Finally, I will re-examine the Gospel's view of the death of Jesus. Käsemann drew heavy criticism for his assertion that in Johannine theology the passion is "a mere postscript which had to be included because John could not ignore this tradition nor yet could he fit it organically into his work."[19] Indeed if the Gospel's Christology does border on Docetism, depicting Jesus as "God on earth" untouched by the realities of human existence, then the death of Jesus fits awkwardly. Exegetes writing since the publication of *The Testament of Jesus* have endeavored to establish that the passion plays a much larger role in Johannine theology and have also sought to correlate more closely the incarnation, ministry, and death of Jesus. The death of Jesus should not be viewed as an ill-fitting addendum, but as the fitting climax of the ministry on earth of the one who "became flesh."

What I offer here, then, is an exegetical reassessment of four

topics: Jesus' origins, incarnation and flesh, signs, and death.
Whereas Käsemann interprets the Gospel from the peculiarly Johannine vantage point of chapter 17, I view the whole Gospel as
the context for establishing what is representative of "Johannine"
theology. This does not eliminate the possibility that there are dis-
tinct layers of tradition in the Gospel, nor that certain parts (e.g.
chap. 21) might have been added after the Gospel was substantially
in its present shape. While acknowledging such a literary history,
scholars have nevertheless increasingly insisted that John 1—21
must be interpreted as a unit. Marinus de Jonge, for instance, writes:

> Behind the present studies lies the assumption that the Fourth Gospel
> is a meaningful whole, highly complicated in structure, with many
> paradoxes and many tensions in thought and syntax, but yet asking
> to be taken seriously as a (more or less) finished literary product in
> which consistent lines of thought can be detected. The possibility of
> development in thought and ways of expression cannot be excluded
> and a long literary process with different stages of redaction may lie
> behind the present Gospel. Yet the first task of an exegete should be
> to interpret the documents as they lie before him.[20]

Perhaps the most vocal proponent of interpreting John 1:1—
21:25 as a coherent literary unity in its present form is Hartwig
Thyen. Thyen eyes with skepticism the attempts to distinguish
sources behind the Gospel and proposes instead a consistently redaction-critical approach that takes all elements within the Gospel
as integral parts of it.[21] In exegeting John, one must offer a synthetic
interpretation of the whole Gospel as a coherent text.[22] The literary-
critical study of the Gospel offered by R. Alan Culpepper also takes
as its subject "the gospel as it stands rather than its sources, historical background, or themes."[23] While the Gospel's integrity is
the starting point of Culpepper's study, it is also its result; from
his analysis of the narrator's point of view he concludes, "In its
present form, if not in its origin, the gospel must be approached as
a unity, a literary whole."[24]

SUMMARY

In sum, I intend to investigate once more the meaning of John
1:14 and the humanity of Jesus in the Fourth Gospel in light of

recent scholarship dealing with that verse in particular and the Gospel as a whole. From the outset certain questions are eliminated:

1. The object of study is the Fourth Gospel. Although the Johannine Epistles strongly hint of a controversy swirling around the significance of Jesus' coming "in the flesh," they will not be considered here. Their inclusion would be justified and expected if my topic were the humanity of Jesus in the Johannine community. For Johannine Christology, one must study the Gospel first.

2. Although John's Christology is often described vis-à-vis Gnosticism, the vexed and complicated question of John's relationship to Gnosticism will not be considered here. Only when the contours of John's portrait of Jesus have been secured would a comparison with gnostic documents be in order; otherwise, one runs the risk of "parallelomania," matching up isolated terms or concepts apart from their setting in their total context.[25]

3. The subject of this investigation is not the "historical Jesus." In considering the "humanity of Jesus," we are not inquiring into the historical veracity of or the tradition behind the Gospel's portrait of Jesus or of the Gospel itself. Neither are we concerned primarily with delineating the relationship of faith and history in John's viewpoint. John's perspective on Jesus' life must surely be taken into consideration, but it is not the focal point of inquiry here.[26]

4. This is not a study of the relationship of John's view of Jesus to later dogmatic formulations. The phrase "humanity of Jesus" inevitably calls to mind the Chalcedonian definition and the question of its relationship to the New Testament and the Fourth Gospel in particular. But these issues are not the subject of the present study.[27] Unquestionably the Fourth Gospel calls Jesus "God,"[28] an appellation that in itself has often made the "humanity of Jesus" in John seem to be an impossible assertion. Whether that is necessarily so remains to be seen.

CHAPTER ONE

THE ORIGINS
OF JESUS

THE PROBLEM OF JESUS' ORIGINS

If, as stated in the introduction, there are essential moments such as birth and death in any human life, then it is natural to begin at the beginning in investigating those moments and hence that life. In ascertaining the Fourth Gospel's view of Jesus' humanity, it is natural, therefore, to begin with the question of his human origins and to ask what the Fourth Gospel says about his parents, heritage, birth, and homeland. Such statements do indeed exist, but they tend to make the question more, not less, complex, inasmuch as they appear as indirect allusions (1:45), on the lips of unbelievers (6:41–42), or as the occasion of dispute (7:40–52). As a result, it is difficult to determine what the evangelist affirms, as opposed to what he presents as falsely held assumptions, about Jesus. Does the evangelist agree with the "Jews who murmured" that Jesus is "the son of Joseph, whose father and mother we know" (6:42)? Or does he introduce such an assessment ironically, as a supreme example of misunderstanding or unbelief? Clearly the denial that Jesus "has come down from heaven" springs from unbelief. But is unbelief also mistaken about Jesus' human heritage?

Complicating the interpretation of those somewhat enigmatic statements about Jesus' human origins are the many forceful and direct statements that Jesus has come "from above," from God, and that he is "not of this world" (e.g. 8:23, 42). In order to assess what the Gospel says about Jesus' origins, the relationship of two sets of statements—those that treat Jesus' origins from heaven and those that treat his earthly origins—must be determined. Are they two truths held in dialectical tension? Or does one set of affirmations inevitably take precedence over the other, so that the statement that Jesus is "from heaven" renders impossible the belief that he is also "son of Joseph"? Nowhere does the Gospel tell us plainly how these statements relate. Instead, what is clear is that Jesus' origins provoke controversy, unbelief, and puzzlement. On almost every page of the Gospel there are traces of the controversy whether Jesus rightly claims to be from God (e.g. 3:2; 7:17; 8:42, 47; 9:16, 33; 13:3) and thus whether he is the divinely sent emissary. Not all agree with this assessment of Jesus. And that disagreement often springs from the offense occasioned by Jesus' apparently all too ordinary heritage.

Rudolf Bultmann agreed that Jesus' human heritage was offensive to "the Jews."[1] Yet he argued that the evangelist not only accepted the facts of Jesus' human origins, but that he took pains to emphasize them precisely because they raise the paradox of Jesus' person. Bultmann writes:

> 'The Jews', knowing Jesus' place of origin and his parents (7:27f.; 6:42) are not in error as to the facts, but err in denying the claim of this Jesus of Nazareth to be the Revealer of God. They err not in the matter upon which they judge but in making a judgment at all *kata sarka* (according to the 'flesh'—according to external appearances).[2]

On Bultmann's terms, although Jesus' human origins are an offense, they do not negate his claim to be the Revealer of God.

And yet throughout the Gospel it is precisely Jesus' origins which are offered as the sure objection against his heavenly origins, indicating that in the minds of many these human origins do preclude Jesus' claims to have "come down from heaven." The various objections can be summed up to make the problem explicit:

1. He is a man: how can he make himself equal to God? (5:18; 10:33)
2. We know his parents: how can he be from heaven? (6:41–42)
3. We know his origins: how can he be the Messiah? (7:27)

4. He comes from Galilee: how can he be the Messiah? (7:41)
5. We do not know where he comes from: how can he be a prophet? (9:29)

In each instance cited above, a perception (e.g. "we know"; "we do not know") expresses the objection to Jesus' messianic status or divine origin. Thus, for Jesus' opponents, the first statement precludes the acceptance of the second: he is a man, therefore, he is not from God; we know his parents, therefore, he cannot have come down from heaven. How the evangelist treats these apparent antitheses is the issue. Does he argue that Jesus is not a man, or that his parents are not known by the crowds, and that therefore the very things which the people dispute are in fact true? If so, what are the implications for Jesus' "real humanity," as the evangelist construes it? Or does the evangelist instead criticize the conclusions that the crowds draw from statements with which he agrees, as Bultmann contends? Again, the question is how these two realities, which the crowds view as mutually exclusive, relate.

Before us, then, is the task of determining the Fourth Gospel's understanding of Jesus' origins by examining the relationship of the statements about Jesus' earthly origins to statements about his heavenly origins. Bultmann argued that John emphasizes the facts about Jesus' human heritage as part of the offense of the incarnation. But Luise Schottroff has both challenged Bultmann and made the question more acute by stating that the problem is not that Jesus' human origins are offensive, but rather that they are simply not relevant to the believer's assessment of him![3] The problem is not that Jesus is not fully human; his human origins are real. But the Fourth Gospel simply does not attach any significance to the realities of this world, including the reality of Jesus' human origins.

The implications of Schottroff's position are clear. If the Fourth Gospel is understood to deny the significance of Jesus' earthly origins, then all the emphasis falls on Jesus' divine or other-worldly origins. And if this were the case, then Jesus' humanity would not be judged a factor significant to genuine faith. But if a more positive evaluation of Jesus' human origins, of his origins within this world, can be established, then the reality and importance of Jesus' humanity are implied. Thus by examining the various texts about Jesus' origins and the disputes surrounding them, we hope to gain insights into the Gospel's understanding of Jesus' earthly origins and their relationship to his origin from above, and so also of the Fourth Gospel's view of the humanity of Jesus.

JESUS' HOMELAND AND GALILEAN ORIGINS

"Can anything good come out of Nazareth?"

The *prima facie* evidence of the Fourth Gospel is that Jesus hails from Galilee (1:45–46; 2:1; 4:43–45; 7:1–9; 7:41–44; 18:5, 7; 19:19). And yet Jesus' Galilean origins are a stumbling block to acceptance of his claims, since Galilee is the home neither of the expected prophet nor of the Messiah (7:41–43; 7:52). Nathanael's innocent ridiculing of Philip's claim to have found the Messiah[4] appears at first to fit this pattern. Philip's announcement that they have found the promised one (1:45) elicits from Nathanael the objection "Can anything good come out of Nazareth?" (1:46). Some commentators assert that the objection here—at least in the eyes of the fourth evangelist—is an objection to Jesus' Galilean origins which make it impossible that he should be the Messiah (cp. 7:41).[5]

Bultmann, however, maintained that what is at issue in Nathanael's objection is the insignificance of Nazareth: that the Messiah comes from Nazareth is part of the offense of the incarnation.[6] Similar is Rudolf Schnackenburg's view that 1:46 is not like 7:41 and 7:52, where Jesus' Galilean origins prevent belief in him as the Messiah or the Prophet, but is rather akin to 6:42, where the Jews murmur about Jesus' statement that he has "come down from heaven," since he is simply "Jesus, the son of Joseph, whose father and mother we know." In both 1:46 and 6:42, Jesus' parents are named specifically ("Jesus of Nazareth, the son of Joseph"; "Jesus, the son of Joseph, whose mother and father we know"). Thus "Can anything good come out of Nazareth?" manifests misgivings about the inauspicious origins of this putative Messiah.[7]

Such misgivings are overcome by faith. The answer to Nathanael's rhetorical question is an invitation to "come and see," a "seeing" which quickly leads to a confession "You are the Son of God! You are the King of Israel!" Jesus responds to Nathanael's confession with the promise that the disciple will "see greater things" (1:50). Within the context of the Gospel, Nathanael's confession rests on Jesus' manifestation of his prophetic knowledge. But the reader's acknowledgment of Nathanael's confession has already received confirmation in the prologue of the Gospel.[8] When one reads of the encounter between Jesus and Nathanael one is scarcely surprised by Nathanael's sudden about-face, for Jesus has already been presented as the Word from above. In this particular instance, any possible conflict between two realities—Nazareth and the Messiah—is reconciled in the community's confession that "the Word became flesh" (1:14). He who is known as "son of Joseph" is also the "Son of God, the King of Israel."

John 4:43–45: A Prophet's Honor in His Own Country

Perhaps one of the most curious and problematic passages in the Fourth Gospel regarding Jesus' origins is 4:43–45. Quite simply, the pericope raises problems because it suggests that Jesus went to Galilee (4:43; cp. 4:1–3) apparently expecting he would receive no honor, "for Jesus himself testified that a prophet has no honor in his own country" (4:44). Very enigmatic, then, is the statement in 4:45: "Therefore when he came to Galilee, the Galileans *welcomed* him, having seen all that he had done in Jerusalem at the feast, for they too had gone to the feast." Because of the difficulty of reconciling vv. 44 and 45, and Jesus' expectation that there would be no honor with the welcome of the Galileans, many scholars conclude that in John, Jesus' "own country" cannot be Galilee, where he *does* receive honor, but must be Judea, where he does not.

Among those who argue that Jesus' own country is Galilee are Brown, Bultmann, Haenchen and Schnackenburg.[9] Bultmann states that *patris* cannot mean Judea because of passages such as 1:46; 7:41; and 7:52; which, taken at face value, assert that Jesus is the "son of Joseph, from Nazareth."[10] He attempts to resolve the apparent contradictions between 4:44 and 4:45 by noting, first, that the evangelist inserted the parenthetical comment (4:44) not to explain Jesus' actual continuing of his journey, but to note that at one time Jesus had spoken this statement about prophets, a statement which is now to be fulfilled. The note is not an element of the chronological framework. Bultmann then observes that the recognition Jesus receives in Galilee is "not true recognition, just as the faith of the people of Jerusalem (2:23) was not true faith."

Among those who suggest that in the Fourth Gospel *patris* refers to Judea (or Jerusalem) are Barrett, de Jonge, Dodd, R. Fortna, Hoskyns, Lindars, and D. M. Smith. They argue that 4:43–45, because it shows the Galileans welcoming Jesus, must be interpreted to mean that Judea is the *patris* which does not honor the prophet. Brown[11] lists three objections to this viewpoint. First, elsewhere in the Fourth Gospel Jesus is apparently from Nazareth in Galilee, a fact which seems to be stressed to a degree not found in the Synoptics. Second, an allusion to Judea would have followed more naturally upon Jesus' departure from that province. Third, if 4:44 is a reference to Judea, then the verse suggests that Jesus came to Galilee in order to receive glory, an idea which is abhorrent to the fourth evangelist (2:24–25; 5:41–44).

These verses imply a contrast not between Galilee and Judea, but between Galilee and Samaria, which had confessed Jesus as "Savior of the world." In spite of his acclamation in Samaria, Jesus moves on to Galilee, knowing full well that his fate there will be rejection. Galilee is certainly not the land where Jesus receives honor, inasmuch as his reception there climaxes in the murmuring of the people and desertion of some of his disciples following the feeding of the five thousand.[12] Yet elsewhere in the Gospel Jesus does not recoil from the judgment which his ministry affects (5:22, 24; 9:39; 12:31). The judgment which arises from unbelief is an inevitable function of his mission. That rejection has already been foreshadowed by the prologue of the Gospel (1:11) and will be summarized in 12:37–40. In this summary, those who do not believe include pilgrims who have come to the feast (12:12) and who have seen "many signs"; presumably Galileans are included in their number. Together these factors suggest that although 4:44 remains a difficult and puzzling verse, it does not deny what is asserted elsewhere in the Gospel: Jesus does indeed hail from Galilee.

John 7:27–28: The Hidden Messiah

The objections against Jesus' origins appear in various forms. It is often observed that the objection of the Jews at 7:27 is an allusion to the Jewish "doctrine" of the "hidden Messiah."[13] Typically the exposition of 7:27–28 runs as follows: The Jews state that Jesus cannot be the Messiah since his origins (presumably Galilean: 6:42; 7:41–42) are common knowledge, whereas the origins of the Messiah, according to the theory of the "hidden Messiah," must be unknown. Jesus' answer, however, indicates that the Jews err in supposing they know where he is from. He is from God; this the Jews do *not* know. Jesus' origins are indeed *unknown* and he does fulfill the requirement "when the Messiah comes, no one will know where he is from." He can, therefore, be the Messiah insofar as that depends upon meeting this particular requirement of Jewish expectations.

Those who suggest that John appeals to the theory of "the hidden Messiah" find this view attested in several of the Pseudepigrapha.[14] In *2 Bar.* 29:3 we read of the time "when the Anointed One shall begin to be revealed" (cp. 39:7; *4 Ezra* 7:28). In a similar vein, *4 Ezra* 13:32 states, "And when these things come to pass and the signs occur which I showed you before, then my son will be revealed." But the contrast between hidden and revealed places the emphasis on God's action in revealing his chosen one, making clear that only God can manifest him whom he anointed. God's Messiah is hidden until the appointed time of his revelation (*4 Ezra* 13:26, 52; *1 Enoch* 48:6; 62:7). It is true that certain passages (*1 Enoch* 48:6; 62:7) speak of the place of the Messiah's concealment: "For this purpose he became the Chosen One; he was concealed in the presence of (the Lord of the Spirits) prior to the creation of the world, and for eternity" (*1 Enoch* 48:6). The passage, however, continues, "And he has *revealed* the wisdom of the Lord of the Spirits to the righteous and the holy ones." Again, the contrast is between the concealment and revelation of the Chosen One.

J. C. O'Neill also points to the rabbinic evidence of *Pirqe Mash-*

iach that God alone has the authority to crown and present his chosen Messiah:

> In that hour [after the Gentile nations have been overthrown by God] God will crown the Messiah and set the helmet of salvation on his head, and will bestow light and glory on him and deck him with garments of honor and set him on a high mountain to bring good news to Israel. And he will proclaim with his voice, Salvation is near! Then the Israelites will say, Who are you? And he will answer, I am Ephraim. And the Israelites will say, Are you he whom God has named: Ephraim, he is my first-born; Is Ephraim my dear son? And he will answer them, Yes.[15]

As O'Neill points out, what is of significance here is that "the Messiah does not admit his identity until God has crowned him, and even then he does so enigmatically. The time of the Messiah is known to God alone."[16]

In Justin Martyr's *Dialogue with Trypho*, there is evidence of a slightly different view. Trypho states: "If indeed the Messiah has been born and exists somewhere, he is unknown, and neither recognizes himself, nor has any power, until Elijah comes and anoints him and makes him manifest to all."[17] Apparently Trypho's contention is that Elijah must reveal the Messiah, and until that revealing occurs, the Messiah, although he may even now be living, is unknown. Again the emphasis falls on the necessity of the revelation of the Messiah so that he can be known. In none of the passages surveyed is there any speculation about where the Messiah is hidden. Indeed, in *1 Enoch* it is assumed that he is with God. Nor is there a hint that his origins are or must be unknown. Rather, the Messiah will be kept by God until the proper time (*2 Bar.* 72:2; *1 Enoch* 48:6; 62:7; see also *Pss. Sol.* 17:21) and when he is revealed, it will be clear that if indeed he is the Messiah, then he also comes from God.

But it is not at all clear that John 7:27 is a definite parallel to the view of the "hidden Messiah."[18] The sudden appearing of the Messiah and his previously hidden state do not seem to lead naturally to the conclusion that the Messiah's origin is unknown; what is unknown is the identity of the Messiah, who he is, as well as the time of his manifestation. Thus there seems to be a clearer allusion

to the view of the "hidden Messiah" in the testimony of John the
Baptist: "I myself *did not know* him; but for this I came baptizing
with water, that he might be *revealed* to Israel" (1:31; cp. 1:26,
"Among you stands one whom you do not know"). While one could
presumably argue that since the identity of the Messiah is unknown,
it follows that his place of origin is unknown, this is not explicitly
spelled out in the extant literature and is not necessarily naturally
derived from the Messiah's hidden identity. Although the Messiah's
whereabouts are not known before he is revealed, there is nothing
to suggest that his origins cannot or will not be known.

A second problem in the exegesis of John 7:27–28 outlined above
is that it depends on the assumption that John is answering a Jewish
objection that Jesus can be the Messiah by showing how he does
in fact fulfill (at least one strand of) Jewish messianic expectation.
Jesus' answer to the Jews points out their folly in assuming they
know "where he is from." What they do not know is that he is
from heaven or from God. But the one thing that is clear about the
Messiah is precisely that he is from God! Before his manifestation
he is hidden by God, he is chosen and anointed by God, and he
will be revealed by God. He is "the Lord's Messiah." Even though
he is "hidden" he is "from God," and "hiddenness" is never contrasted with his commissioning or anointing by God. It thus seems
odd to suggest that John is arguing that Jesus fulfills the qualifications of the Messiah because he is from God. It is precisely the
source of Jesus' authority—whether he is from God—that is at issue
in John. But the acceptance of Jesus' authority is a problem not of
Jesus' fulfilling the proper messianic role, but of the stubbornness
of unbelievers in accepting the witnesses that testify to Jesus.
Whereas the unbeliever demands certain qualifications in the one
who is the Messiah that would prove he is from God, Jesus asserts
that he is from God, something which those who judge by earthly
standards can never see (7:24; cp. 8:15). What is at issue in 7:27,
then, is not whether Jesus meets a specific qualification for messiahship, but the unbelief of Jesus' opponents: "he who sent me is
true, and him you do not know." If they knew God, they would
know his Messiah.

The most likely conclusion to be drawn here is that if John intends to address himself to a specific Jewish objection to Jesus' messianic status, then that objection rests on a Jewish belief for which neither the pseudepigraphal materials nor Justin's dialogue provides an exact parallel.[19] Either John has knowledge of a related but different strain of the tradition of the "unknown Messiah," or he has formulated the Jewish objection in accordance with the belief attested throughout the Gospel that the nub of the problem is the refusal of the Jews to believe Jesus' claim to come from God. This does not imply that the fourth evangelist has no interest in Jewish messianic expectations. There is ample evidence elsewhere in the Gospel to show that he believes Jesus does fulfill the role of Messiah and that this person is a specifically Jewish figure. But John's treatment of the objections here (7:27–28) underscores his belief that even were Jesus to answer satisfactorily all those objections, that would still not lead inevitably to belief in him. Rather, traditional expectations must be set aside insofar as they encourage judgment according to external standards (7:24). The discussion regarding Jesus' origins in 7:27–28 is paradigmatic of that external judgment and hence of the failure to comprehend Jesus.

John 7:41–42, 52: "Is the Messiah to come from Galilee?"

While the dispute in John 7:25–31 is about the Messiah and his origins, Galilee is not named specifically since the problem of those origins is discussed in terms of belief and unbelief in Jesus' ultimate authority. At 7:41–42 and 7:52 there is a specific complaint that Jesus' Galilean origins preclude his claim to messiahship. The scene is set at Tabernacles. Following Jesus' words on the last day of the feast, some of the people acclaim him as "the Prophet" (7:40) while others acknowledge him as Messiah (7:41).[20]

In each case, however, there is an objection based on Jesus' Galilean origins. Whereas some claim Jesus is the Messiah (7:40), others raise the scriptural objection that the Messiah "is descended from David, and comes from Bethlehem, the city where David was" (7:43). The evangelist remarks "so there was a division among the people over him." Obviously some were willing to confess Jesus as the Messiah despite his Galilean heritage. At 7:50, Nicodemus is found as a supporter of Jesus and urges not that Jesus' heritage be reviewed, but rather that his words and deeds form the basis for any judgments passed upon him. The Pharisees, however, answer in terms of scriptural proof texts: "Search and you will see that no prophet is to rise from Galilee."

Barrett is not alone in suggesting that the evangelist alludes here to Jesus' birth in Bethlehem.[21] If there is an unspoken reference to the birth at Bethlehem, then Jesus indeed meets the demands of the proof text. The Pharisees who think that neither the Messiah nor the Prophet can come from Galilee fail to recognize that Jesus fulfills both roles and is, in fact, not from Galilee at all. Yet it is curious that the statements about Jesus' heritage and Galilean origins are always on the lips of Jesus' opponents and are never explicitly refuted: the objections are presented, but never answered. Thus to the query "Has not the scripture said that the Christ is descended from David, and comes from Bethlehem, the village where David was?" (7:42) the evangelist offers neither a refutation nor any proof that Jesus was truly from Bethlehem. Instead, he comments, "So there was a division among the people over him" (7:43). Likewise, in 7:48 the Pharisees expostulate with the officers that none of the authorities has believed in Jesus. But no response is offered to their demand that Nicodemus search the law (7:51–52). Clearly the evangelist is more concerned to delineate the variety of responses to Jesus and the division between believers and unbelievers than to answer the question "How can these things be?"[22]

THE PROBLEM OF JESUS' BIRTH
AND PARENTS

"Is not this Jesus, the son of Joseph?"

Closely related to the question of Jesus' geographical origins is the question of the meaning of the designation "son of Joseph." In 1:45 Philip speaks of Jesus as "the son of Joseph," as do the Jews in 6:42. Barrett believes that John likely knows the tradition of the virgin birth: "It is in accord with his ironical use of traditional material that he should allow Jesus to be ignorantly described as 'son of Joseph' while himself believing that Jesus had no human father."[23] He allows the designation "son of Joseph" to underscore the mistake of the Jews, for had they known the truth of Jesus' parentage they would not have rejected his claim to have come from heaven. "Son of Joseph" thus stands over against the claim of Jesus' heavenly origins in the mind of the Jews, but not in the thought of the evangelist, since for him Jesus is in fact not the "son of Joseph" at all. John's answer is given in terms of the virgin birth, a fact which would be known to John's Christian readers.

On the other hand, C. H. Dodd argues that 1:45 constitutes a formal confession of the Messiah by Philip, and as such can hardly be understood as a case of mistaken identity.[24] In fact, it is the evangelist's intention to designate Jesus as "son of Joseph," and then to ascribe to him certain Christological titles (Messiah, Son of God, King of Israel, Son of man). Certainly the programmatic character of the messianic witness of chapter 1 of the Gospel has been amply demonstrated.[25] And not only does chapter 1 bear witness to the identity of Jesus, but it also does so within the context of the calling of the first disciples and their initial confessions of faith. After his calling, Andrew (1:39) tells Simon Peter that Jesus is the Messiah (1:41); similarly, after his calling, Philip (1:43) confesses Jesus as the one promised in Scripture (1:45). And when Nathanael is told to "come and see," he exclaims that Jesus is the Son of God, the King of Israel. Finally, Jesus himself speaks of the Son of man. As Dodd comments:

> These titles [are] understood, not as contradicting Philip's description of His human identity, but as affirming that He who is, on the human plane, "Jesus son of Joseph" is *also* that which these titles imply. It is this "and also" that raises the Christological problem, as John conceives it, and his doctrine of the Incarnation is the answer.[26]

Dodd's statement points out that the problem regarding Jesus' identity in the Fourth Gospel concerns the relationship of Jesus' earthly origins or identity—"Jesus of Nazareth, the son of Joseph"—to his origin from above. The solution can be formulated in several ways. As Barrett states it, the heavenly origin of Jesus rules out the possibility that he is also from earth; that is, that Jesus is "Son of God" makes it impossible that one can view him as "son of Joseph." Jesus' heavenly and earthly origins are mutually exclusive, formulated as an either/or statement. But as Dodd views the problem, the answer is not an either/or. That Jesus is from heaven does not necessarily imply that he is not also "the son of Joseph."[27]

John 8:31–59: Offspring and Children of Abraham

Jesus' debate with "the Jews" in chapter 8 suggests a resolution of the problem of Jesus' origins. Beginning especially with 8:31, a bitter controversy is recounted between Jesus and his opponents about their origins and heritage. Jesus grants the Jews their claim that they are offspring of Abraham (8:37). They are physically descended from Abraham, but physical descent is not the ultimate criterion in discerning their relationship to their father. What is important is conduct: to show themselves to be Abraham's children, the Jews ought to do what he did.[28] By this test, although the Jews are *offspring* of Abraham, they are not truly *children* of Abraham. Similarly, by implication, the true "children of Abraham" are not necessarily only those who are his offspring. Thus there is disjunction between one's physical descent or origin and one's true identity.[29] One's physical or earthly origins are not the ultimate definition of identity.

Nevertheless, earthly origins are not insignificant. Elsewhere in the Gospel it is clear that "salvation is from the Jews" (4:22) and that to understand the Law and Moses means to become a disciple of Jesus. The implications of one's earthly origins can and must be brought to fruition in the sphere of faith. In this instance, fulfillment for the Jews who claim Abrahamic descent would mean to remain faithful to the word of Jesus, the Son who is able to grant them true freedom (8:34–36). Jesus does not repudiate Abraham or his descendants. Abraham's joyous acceptance of the Messiah becomes the paradigmatic response which the Jewish people ought also to manifest. Similarly, though the blind man who is healed in chapter 9 is shunned by his parents and rejected by the Pharisees, such rejection does not imply that the man's earthly heritage was a hindrance to his confession of faith, for it is quite clear that the Pharisees too should have made the confession which he made (9:40–

41). One's identity does not ultimately depend upon one's earthly heritage, but neither does it negate either the existence or importance of the earthly sphere.

In sum, while it is true for the Fourth Gospel that one's true identity is not determined by one's physical origins, the Gospel does not imply that these origins are no longer relevant. In fact, to the contrary, in both chapters 8 and 9 it is clear that the Jews should have brought their natural heritage to fruition in the confession of Jesus as Messiah. Similarly, although the prologue states that the children of God are those who were born "not of blood nor of the will of the flesh nor of the will of man, but of God" (1:13; 3:3), such "divine birth" or heavenly origin in no way means that one's earthly origins are either irrelevant or an impediment to true faith.[30] Rather, "his own" should have received him and thus shown themselves to be "children of God" (1:13; 8:39, 42, 44). So, although the Jews claim to be offspring of Abraham (8:39) and children of God (8:41), they are not in fact children of God, because they do not do his will (8:40–41, 44); while Jesus, the "son of Joseph" is truly the Son of the Father (8:42, 47, 49) because he honors the Father (8:49–50, 54).[31] Just as the Jews need not deny their heritage from Abraham to be disciples of Jesus and, hence, true children of God, so those who do not believe that Jesus is Messiah or Son of God cannot appeal to the designation "son of Joseph" as negative evidence.

THE COMMUNITY'S CONFESSION OF FAITH

According to the Fourth Gospel, realities that are mutually exclusive for unbelievers are not so for the believing community. On the one hand, unbelievers object that *because* they know Jesus' parents, he cannot be from God; *because* they know his origins, he cannot be the Messiah. It is not their *perception*—"we know his parents"—which is criticized, but the *conclusion* which they draw from it—"he is not from God." On the other hand, for believers there is no hindrance to confessing Jesus as the promised one (1:45) and the "one who has come down from heaven" (6:42), even though there are no readily available arguments to counteract charges that he is simply "the son of Joseph." Philip's confession (1:45), and the steadfastness of those disciples who do not fall away (6:66–69), show that faith holds these two realities together. That Jesus hails from Nazareth or Galilee is a stumbling block to some, but faith overcomes the offense (1:46; 6:69, "we have believed"). Thus the evangelist does not dispute Jesus' Galilean origins or his earthly parentage, nor does he answer all Jewish objections against Jesus' messiahship. Instead, it appears that he lets them stand.

The Evangelist's Method of Argumentation

But one must ask, "Why does the evangelist let the facts stand?"[32] Perhaps he does not agree with them, but in his ironical allusions to the virgin birth and to Jesus' birth in Bethlehem he actually rejects the so-called facts of Jesus' human heritage. That the Gospel even alludes to these problems suggests this possibility. Why raise charges for which there are no adequate responses? Nevertheless, it is still puzzling that the Gospel offers no direct or explicit evidence against the charges. It does not include traditions similar to the birth narratives of Matthew and Luke, for example, which would constitute such evidence.

With respect to John's knowledge of these traditions, there are a number of alternatives possible. One could argue that John knows them but disapproves of or disagrees with them, that he does not know them at all, or that he knows and accepts but does not comment on them.[33] Adopting the latter view implies that Christian readers, who would be acquainted with the tradition of the virgin birth and the birth in Bethlehem, would supply the proper responses at the appropriate points to Jewish objectors. But as Meeks points out, to speak of the irony of 7:41, 52, for example, presupposes the Fourth Gospel's acquaintance with the Synoptics, or, at least with traditions very much like them.[34] Johannine dependence on the Synoptics, however, is a datum which is neither proved nor necessary. And although we may well appeal to John's general acquaintance with Synoptic-like tradition, there is no way of knowing whether that included traditions paralleling the first two chapters of Matthew and Luke.

Moreover, if by referring to Jesus as the "son of Joseph" the

evangelist intends for his readers to recognize the irony because
they know of the virgin birth, then that irony depends on infor-
mation not available elsewhere in the Gospel. Although that possibility cannot be dismissed, it would be atypical of the evangelist's
method; usually he clarifies misunderstandings elsewhere in the
Gospel.[35] In short, it is not clear that the Fourth Gospel advances
its argument by appealing to the virgin birth or to the birth in
Bethlehem. The argument for Jesus' identity in John is not an ex-
tended apologetic against the various charges made against his
human origins. To this extent, one can agree with Bultmann and
Wengst that the evangelist "lets the facts stand."

But again we face the question "Why does the evangelist present
the argument in this way?" Throughout the Gospel the question of
Jesus' origins and, hence, of his identity, is the source of continual
friction and debate. Why is no more definitive "proof" offered?
Why are the counter arguments not presented succinctly and directly? Bultmann suggested that the evangelist wished both to underscore the offense of the Revealer's humanity and to evoke faith
(which can never rest on proof) in him. On this point, recent analyses of the situation lying behind the Fourth Gospel are instructive.[36] If the Gospel reflects a situation in which Jewish Christians
are facing or have faced exclusion from the Jewish majority because
of their messianic confession, then it makes little sense for the evangelist to confront believers with the offense of Jesus' person. The
offense of Jesus' messiahship was amply demonstrated by the community's opponents![37]

The Problem of Belief and Unbelief

If we do not have definitive refutations of those opponents'
charges in the Gospel, what we do have is the community's confession of faith and the roll call of the witnesses to Jesus' identity.
There is the inaugural witness of John at the Jordan. There are the
confessions of the first disciples (chap. 1) and of the Samaritan
woman and her townsfolk. In chapter 9 the question of Jesus'
origins arises in the controversy with the blind man whom Jesus
healed. Although chapter 9 is often interpreted as recounting the
expulsion of the healed man from the synagogue for confessing that

Jesus is the Messiah, nevertheless nowhere in 9:1–41 does anyone actually make such a confession. When the account is read without the parenthetical vv. 22–23 (perhaps a later insertion), the dispute clearly centers on whether Jesus comes from God (9:16, 29, 30–31). It is really the question of Jesus' origins, not whether he is the Messiah, which underlies this narrative. Only the healed man, who makes a confession of faith ("Lord, I believe," 9:38), recognizes that Jesus comes from God (9:30). In this respect the healing and dispute which follow it are clear parallels to the healing and discourse in chapter 5, where Jesus' authority, given to him by the Father who sent him (vv. 36–37), is accepted only by those who believe (vv. 38, 40, 43).

The confessions of Jesus as the Word made flesh, Messiah, Son of God, Son of man, and so on, disclose what is at stake for the evangelist. It is this estimation of Jesus for which the evangelist contends. Thus he stresses Jesus' origins "from above." Because of this emphasis, one might expect a concomitant reticence to speak of Jesus' earthly heritage. But this is not the case. Even though these origins are the cause of doubt and unbelief, John never rebuts the objections against Jesus. Indeed, he regularly alludes to Jesus' geographical homeland and human parentage precisely in settings where they are the source of conflict and controversy. In the course of these various debates, the offense of Jesus' human origins is apparently neither lessened nor removed. Rather, Jesus' discourses and debates with the Jews accentuate the distinction between those who do not reject Jesus and those who do. By allowing Jesus' opponents to raise objections and to deny his heavenly origins on the basis of his earthly origins, the Gospel underscores the obstacles which the would-be believer faces. Some do acclaim him, but the crowds are divided, and most remain tentative, unsure, or openly antagonistic.

Thus the Johannine statements about Jesus' origins show that the failure to recognize and receive the Messiah is due in part to the offense which the unbeliever finds in those earthly origins. Although the Jews do not grasp the secret of Jesus' identity, the reader shares the evangelist's omniscient viewpoint and has access to his "implicit commentary" from the very outset, for John 1:1–18 reveals the

secret that Jesus is the Word from above.[38] In a comparison of the
opening verses of Mark and its "messianic secret" with John 1:1–
18 and the secret of Jesus' identity in John, Morna Hooker observes:

> The faith to which the disciples are called—together with the readers
> of the gospel—is precisely that which is revealed to us in the opening
> verses: and it is precisely this estimate of Jesus which divides disciple
> from unbeliever, for those who do not see and understand the divine
> revelation are those who remain outside, and who are offended by
> what Jesus does. . . . It is certainly true that the messianic secret in
> Mark indicates a tension in the *present* experience of the evangelist
> and his readers: their generation is divided into those who have eyes
> to see and those who have not. The problem is not simply that men
> and women failed to recognize *then* the one whom they *now* ac-
> knowledge to be Messiah; but that the question "Who is he?" can
> still be given totally opposing answers.[39]

The same holds true for the Gospel of John. Here too there is division between those who accept Jesus' claims and those who do
not. But what is hidden in John's Gospel is the truth that Jesus is
"from above," from God. Or, put differently, the problem of the
origins of Jesus divides those inside and those outside the believing
community.

Undoubtedly there is an echo here of the experience of the evangelist and his community. The disputes over Jesus' origins and authority testify that it is the unbelief of the Jews in the Jewish Messiah
which still calls for explanation. "He came unto his own, and his
own received him not" receives continual illustration and explanation throughout the course of the Gospel. And the estimate of
faith which the Gospel seeks to instill is precisely that which is
spelled out in 1:14: "The Word became flesh." How can Jesus, a
man, "make himself equal to God?" How can Jesus, whose parents
are known to all, be from heaven? The answer to these questions
is found in the confession "The Word became flesh." As Hooker
writes, "The most puzzling Johannine discourse is immediately il-
luminated by a re-reading of the Prologue."[40]

SUMMARY

Thus the Gospel's witness to Jesus' earthly origins can be summed
up as follows:

1. The evangelist does not negate the significance of earthly origins, whether those of Jesus or of believers, as the discourse with the Jews in chapter 8 makes clear. But just as the natural heritage of the Jews does not necessarily disclose their ultimate identity, neither does Jesus' earthly heritage sum up or reveal the mystery of his person. Acknowledgment of God's Messiah cannot be deduced from a chain of proof texts.

2. Rather, an acknowledgment of Jesus as the one sent from God grows out of faith, by virtue of which one judges neither by appearance (7:24) nor by the flesh (8:15), but by the Spirit (6:63, 65). The secret of Jesus' origins belongs to the secret of his person, which unbelief does not grasp.[41] But faith overcomes the possible offense of Jesus' earthly origins. Certainly the various disputes in which Jewish authorities introduce proofs that Jesus' origins disqualify his claims show that an academic knowledge of those human origins is insufficient to lead to faith.

3. Finally, faith grasps the truth that Jesus comes from God, a truth voiced in the evangelist's assertion that Jesus is "the Word made flesh." Thus John 1:1–18 provides the indispensable clue to Jesus' origins for the reader of the Gospel, and it is precisely this estimate of Jesus which the evangelist and his community confess: "And the Word became flesh . . . and *we* beheld his glory."

CHAPTER TWO

INCARNATION AND FLESH

Again and again Jesus' human origins raise the question of his identity because of their testimony to his humanity. Yet the words which are quoted most often as disclosing John's understanding of the humanity of Jesus as well as the secret of who he is are "and the Word became flesh" (*kai ho logos sarx egeneto*; John 1:14). At first glance 1:14 scarcely seems open to a wide variety of interpretations: it simply asserts that the divine Word became human (*sarx* = flesh). In broad terms, then, the Gospel witnesses to the "incarnation" of the Word; not even Käsemann denies this. What is at issue is the Gospel's understanding of that incarnation. Recent exegetical discussion has sharpened the focus of the question, casting a critical eye on the exact connotations of the word "flesh" and the resultant implications for interpreting the "enfleshment" of the Word. It is the narrower aspect of the discussion which concerns us here, for John's view of "incarnation" is closely related to his view of Jesus' humanity, inasmuch as it reveals his estimate of Jesus' flesh. What exactly does the Fourth Gospel mean when it says "the Word became *flesh*?" Does the *sarx* of 1:14 demand an incarnation which entails Jesus' unquestioned humanity? Or is it merely a way of asserting that the Word entered into this world, yet only in the guise of flesh, simply disguised as a human being?

THE PROBLEM AND CONTRIBUTIONS OF
RECENT SCHOLARSHIP

Bultmann and Käsemann

Against the backdrop of 1:14, the differences between Bultmann and Käsemann stand out most acutely. Bultmann defined the Johannine view of *sarx* (found in all passages except 6:51–58, which represents the ecclesiastical redactor's conflicting viewpoint) as the human and worldly sphere, which is transitory, illusory, inauthentic, helpless, futile, and corrupting—"the nothingness of man's whole existence."[1] Such an interpretation contributes directly to his view of the incarnation as offense: God has revealed himself precisely in this worldly sphere, in this flesh, and because "the divine is the very counter-pole to the human. . . . it is a paradox, an offense, that the Word became flesh."[2]

Each element of the statement "the Word became flesh" has significance. That the *Logos* is the subject of this statement attests that "revelation is an event with an other-worldly origin"; revelation comes from God and thus the Logos is God in his self-revelation.[3] To affirm that this Logos became *sarx* means that revelation, if it is to have significance for human beings, must take place within the human sphere. Thus the statement "the Word became flesh" means that God's revelation occurs in the human sphere or in the fleshly sphere. Yet it is precisely here that Jesus' contemporaries balk; their natural desire demands that the Revealer's humanity function merely as a transparent disguise through which they can easily see his divinity. It is this fleshly desire which the incarnation does not allow:

All such desires are cut short by the statement: the Word became flesh. It is in his sheer humanity that he is the Revealer. True, his own also see his *doxa* (14b); indeed if it were not to be seen, there would be no grounds for speaking of revelation. But this is the paradox which runs through the whole Gospel: the *doxa* is not to be seen *alongside* the *sarx*, nor *through* the *sarx* as through a window; it is to be seen in the *sarx* and nowhere else. If man wishes to see the *doxa*, then it is on the *sarx* that he must concentrate his attention, without allowing himself to fall a victim to appearances. The revelation is present in a peculiar *hiddenness*.[4]

Because the revelation is present in hiddenness only, "the divinity of the figure of Jesus in John is completely lacking in visibility."[5]

In sum, then, flesh is not material substance; the emphasis of 1:14 falls not on the palpability of the Revealer but rather on his "pure and simple humanity."[6] "The Word became flesh" should not be construed as an anti-docetic attempt to establish the real flesh of the Revealer. Instead, it underscores the theme of John's Gospel, which is at the same time the offense of that Gospel, that the Revealer is a man. In an almost uncanny anticipation of Käsemann's interpretation of these same verses, Bultmann writes:

> Never can faith turn away from [the incarnate one], as if the "glory"—or the "truth" and "life"—could ever become directly visible, or as if the Revelation consisted of a certain thought-content, and the incarnation of the "word" were only a device . . . for transmitting that content.[7]

Käsemann objects that it is precisely this understanding which 1:14 does not allow. John's theme is distilled in 1:14c—"we have beheld his glory"—and the divine glory emanating from the Word greatly overshadows the human flesh in which he "dwelt among us." John depicts not a revealer hidden in flesh, but a glorious "god striding across the earth." It is possible to see God's glory in the incarnate one because incarnation in John can be equated with the manifestation of the Creator on earth: "Incarnation for John is really epiphany."[8]

In support of this argument, Käsemann approvingly cites C. K. Barrett's definition that *sarx* in the Fourth Gospel "stands for humanity over against God." Käsemann continues:

> The implication of this for the exegesis of 1:14 is this: "flesh as [*sic*] the place where the Word of God is recognized." The paradox—and there certainly *is* a paradox—in 1:14a consists in the fact that the Creator enters the world of createdness and in so doing exposes himself to the judgment of the creature. The "presence of God" on earth is the real goal of the becoming flesh. This "presence of God" on earth may be combined with the stumbling block to men, but this does not in any way imply that the becoming flesh as such is the stumbling block.[9]

"Flesh" is merely the channel of God's self-communication to his creatures.[10] "The Word became flesh" (1:14a) provides the presupposition for writing the earthly story of Jesus, but it means no more than the temporary descent of the Logos to the earth in order to mediate contact between the heavenly and earthly realms.[11] The Logos changes his place, but never really changes himself.[12] Käsemann acknowledges that some features of "lowliness" remain attached to the figure of Jesus; these he deems the "minimum costume" necessary for one who is to dwell on earth. But the traces of "lowliness" which linger in the Gospel are characteristic of the earthly realm which the Revealer enters, not of the Revealer himself. Typical characterizations of John's view of the incarnation as "humiliation," "condescension," or "paradox" miss the mark.[13] Indeed, if Bultmann sums up the Gospel's theme as "the Revealer is nothing but a man," then on Käsemann's terms, "the Revealer is God and nothing else."[14]

Luise Schottroff

Käsemann's interpretation of 1:14 and of John's view of *sarx*, vis-à-vis Bultmann, has occasioned considerable discussion. Once again, Luise Schottroff offers quite a different interpretation, charging that neither Bultmann nor Käsemann adequately explained the Johannine view of incarnation, inasmuch as the Gospel insists that the flesh of the Revealer was temporary, fleeting, and therefore irrelevant to faith in him. The Gospel betrays no traces of Docetism, as though Jesus only appeared to be human; he was indeed fully human (against Käsemann), but this fact is meaningless for faith (against Bultmann). In fact, Schottroff argues, the Fourth Gospel views all material realities, and not only the flesh of the Revealer, as irrelevant, for "the flesh profits nothing" (6:63).

Schottroff's position points to a trend in recent scholarship: to insist that John's view of material realities, especially the *sarx* (in 1:14 and elsewhere), is critical in ascertaining the Fourth Gospel's understanding of the humanity of Jesus. By investigating John's view of material realities, and particularly his view of *sarx*, we can better understand what John intended to say when he wrote, "The Word became *flesh*," and, consequently, how he viewed the humanity of Jesus.

Thyen and Richter

Recent Johannine studies have cited the failure of both Bultmann and Käsemann to suggest a concrete *Sitz-im-Leben* for the origin of 1:14: neither explains satisfactorily the historical context which called for this view of Jesus' humanity, whether as a defensive apologetic or a positive creative statement. More than one scholar has endeavored to remedy this lack, thereby hoping better to explain the meaning of 1:14.

We note, for example, the studies of Hartwig Thyen and Georg Richter. Both have written extensively on the prologue. Moreover, each agrees that a particular view of Jesus' humanity is manifested by 1:14 and the way in which it became part of the prologue in its present form. Thyen argues that 1:14–18 is one of many additions to an original *Grundschrift* (foundational document) by the "anti-docetic" evangelist.[15] According to Thyen, 1:14 stresses the real incarnation of the Logos in Jesus and as such is very consciously anti-docetic. In spite of a growing consensus to the contrary, 1:14b ("and dwelt among us") cannot be understood as a statement about the epiphany of the Creator among human beings (so Käsemann). In fact, 1:14b *contradicts* Käsemann's interpretation of it, since it sharpens 1:14a ("the Word became flesh") through the use of climactic parallelism and stresses the bodily presence of the Logos who lived as a human among humans ("and dwelt among us").[16] Those verses which insist on the identity of the flesh and the Logos (1:14) or the identity of Jesus and the Son of God (20:31) provide the evangelist's answer to his opponents. Since these verses affirm that because of the incarnation the divine Logos, the Son of God, cannot be severed from Jesus of Nazareth, it follows that one must certainly "look at the flesh" to see the revelation of glory. Nevertheless, for the evangelist the accent does not fall on Jesus' "pure and simple humanity."[17] Rather, it falls on the peculiar path which Jesus walked—a path characterized by love for his own which led ultimately to his death—because the question the evangelist faces is whether the Logos is indeed one with Jesus of Nazareth. Inasmuch as the evangelist insists that one must look at the path which Jesus walked to see the revelation of glory, he insists that flesh constitutes an indispensable aspect of that revelation.

By contrast, Richter argues that vv. 14–18 present a tendency that conflicts with the evangelist's explicit intention, found in 20:31, in writing the Gospel. On the one hand, the statement that "Jesus is the Christ, the Son of God," (20:31) stands in the service of the evangelist's desire to prove Jesus' heavenly origins and certainly has no anti-docetic overtones. The claim that Jesus comes from heaven causes offense because of his undisputed humanity and it was, therefore, unnecessary for the evangelist to defend or even emphasize it.[18] On the other hand, what is at issue in 1:14 is Jesus' corporeality, his real humanity; and it was against an anti-docetic faction's denial of these that a later redactor asserted that the Word indeed became "flesh." In short, for Richter the *sarx* of 1:14 can be equated with "human being," and that verse unequivocally upholds Jesus' full humanity. Insofar as they contend that in the Gospel in its present form there is an emphasis on flesh and its role in revelation, Thyen and Richter agree with the broad outlines of Bultmann's interpretation of incarnation and John 1:14.[19] Yet they explain the insertion into the prologue of 1:14 with its emphasis on flesh as a response to quite different but concrete controversies within the Johannine community. By endeavoring to answer the question why 1:14 speaks of the enfleshment of the Word, they hope to offer more convincing explanations of what that enfleshment entails.

Summary

Recent studies have argued persuasively that in order to understand incarnation in John one must deal with the two related problems of the content and purpose of 1:14. Precisely what does the Gospel intend when it says "the Word became flesh," and why does it say what it does? Here the nuance of the word *sarx* is of utmost importance. Does the use of *sarx* in 1:14 (and elsewhere) emphasize the offense of the assertion that God has revealed himself in the transitory, fleshly sphere? Does it represent an anti-docetic insistence on Jesus' corporeality against a denial of its reality? Or is it merely a cipher for depicting God's revelation to his creatures? In order to answer the question of the connotations and use of *sarx* in 1:14 and elsewhere in the Gospel (1:13; 3:6; 6:51–59, 63; 8:15;

17:2), an exegetical examination of each verse is called for. Two procedural notes are in order here: (1) Because 1:14 has received such a disproportionate share of attention, it merits close scrutiny and, hence, a somewhat longer discussion than some of the other verses. (2) Because 6:51–59 is so often assigned to a redactor, not the evangelist, it will be held over until the end of the discussion, after the other uses of *sarx* have been analyzed.

THE MEANING OF *SARX* IN THE FOURTH GOSPEL

Sarx in John 1:13

Bultmann writes that in 1:13 the word "flesh" is used to draw a sharp contrast between one's origins in the human sphere and the possibility of becoming a child of God through the divine act of begetting.[20] While it is certainly true that natural birth and birth from God are contrasted, this contrast is not inherent in the word "flesh." Rather, the contrast arises from the opposition between a series of phrases which characterize natural birth (born of blood, of the will of the flesh, of the will of man) and the twice-repeated phrase "of God," which points to divine birth.[21] By juxtaposing these phrases the evangelist sets the human act of natural, physical birth over against God's activity in spiritual birth. But in itself *sarx* connotes that which is natural or, in this instance, human. "Will of the flesh" could be paraphrased as "human desire" or "human will." Unquestionably there is a contrast between birth effected by the human will and God's own action, and thus *sarx* here connotes "humanity over against God" or "the sphere of the natural, the powerless, the superficial, opposed to the 'spirit.' "[22] But "flesh" itself is basically synonymous with "humanity," the *pasa sarx* of 17:2.

Sarx in John 1:14

In interpreting 1:14, two questions are of particular relevance: (1) What is the meaning of *sarx*? (2) What is the function or purpose of this verse within 1:1–18, the prologue of the Gospel? The function of the verse in its context is important, because when 1:1–18 is read as a narrative, tracing sequentially the revelation in the Word from creation through incarnation, 1:14 is quite often taken as the first reference to the incarnation. As a result, it is also taken as the Gospel's principal and summarizing statement of that incarnation. That the Gospel uses the term *sarx* at this point leads to the conclusions that the term stands in sharp contrast to the predication of the divinity of the Word (1:1–3) and that the flesh of the Word is, in fact, emphasized. It is no surprise that Bultmann, who thinks that 1:14 sums up the theme of the Gospel, also argues that it constitutes a "turning point" within the prologue.[23]

In defining *sarx* in 1:14, Bultmann comments that it stresses the sphere of the human and the worldly "in its transitoriness, helplessness and vanity"; "it is the realm of first appearances"; "it exerts a corrupting power"; "it possesses an illusory form of life."[24] Bultmann virtually equates flesh with humanity: to say that "the Word became flesh" means that "the Revealer is nothing but a man." Nevertheless, his definition of "humanity" carries a very particular meaning which depends more on his existentialism than on the meaning of *sarx* itself.

Certainly in 1:14 *sarx* does stand in contrast to the divine. The evangelist uses the term *Logos* for the first time since the opening lines of the prologue, thus calling attention to the fact that the same Logos who "was with God" and "was God," was the Logos who "became flesh."[25] Not only is there a contrast between the eternal "was" of 1:1 and the historical "became flesh" of 1:14a, but there is also a contrast between the predication that the Logos was "with God" and that he resided "among us."[26] John has in view a difference in the "mode of being" of the Word with God and his residence among human beings.[27] When the two statements—"The Word was with God" and "The Word became flesh"—are placed side by side, the contrast between them is evident. The former predication states that the one who was God dwelt with God; the latter statement can be paraphrased, "The one who became a human being dwelt among human beings." Thus there is no major difference between the connotation of *sarx* in 1:13 and *sarx* in 1:14.[28]

Similarly Käsemann views the peculiar Johannine meaning of

sarx as "humanity over against God." But he argues that *sarx* has the nuance of "creatureliness," the "world of createdness."[29] "The Word became flesh" means that the Creator entered the sphere of createdness. Käsemann argues that 1:14–18 expresses the same truth as 1:9–13, albeit in different terms, and thus describes the Logos' entry into the *kosmos*, which was made through him (cf. 1:3). In the incarnation the Logos does come into the world which was created by God through him. When the Logos enters the world and takes on flesh, he enters the realm of createdness.

Here Käsemann's interpretation depends upon his argument that 1:14a does not constitute a "turning point" within the prologue since vv. 5a, 10a, and 11a already speak of the incarnation.[30] He is not alone in championing this view.[31] In fact, one of the chief contributions of recent studies of the prologue (1:1–18) has been to point out the parallel between vv. 5–13 and 14–18.[32] These two parallel sections describe, in different terms, the encounter of the Logos with a hostile audience (darkness; the world; his own). They do not comprise a sequential narration of revelation before and after the incarnation.[33] Nevertheless, it does not follow, as Käsemann asserts, that 1:14a ("the Word became flesh") states nothing new, but that in light of 1:14c ("we beheld his glory") it merely shows that the flesh served as a passageway for the communication of God with humanity. Simply because these verses (5a, 10a, 11a, and 14a) all refer to the same event does not mean that they do not have different emphases; the becoming flesh is not thereby diminished in importance. There is a narrowing of terms in 1:1–18, so that the presence of the Logos is first described in the world; then among his own people, the Jews; and finally, as one enfleshed, his glory was seen by those who believed in him. The narrowing of terms, however, does not correspond to a narrative of the Logos' activity, as though he were first in the world, then among his own, and finally in the flesh. Rather, 1:1–18 describes the activity of the Logos under different aspects or from differing perspectives.

John 1:14 reiterates what has already been stated in 1:1–18, and it does so in different and appropriate terminology, speaking of the coming of the Logos in the language of those who are themselves flesh (cp. 17:2). Verse 1:14 demands the identity of the Logos and the flesh: only in this manner can he be said to have "dwelt among us," that is, among those who are also flesh. "The Word became flesh" describes the way in which the Word was in the world and in which he came to his own, in which "he dwelt among us."[34] It is only after the prologue asserts that "the Word became flesh" that it also changes from third person ("all who received him," v. 12) to first person (v. 14). The confessional "we beheld his glory" (1:14c), which refers first of all to the "seeing" of eye-witnesses, follows naturally upon the assertions in 1:14ab.[35] Because the Word became flesh, the way is opened to beholding and testifying to his glory.

Sarx in John 3:6

Whereas Käsemann assigns the flesh/spirit antithesis of 3:6 to a Hellenistic dualism uncharacteristic of the evangelist,[36] many scholars take it as the starting point for interpreting *sarx* in the rest of the Gospel. Bultmann, for example, consistently refers to 3:6 (and 6:63) as characteristic of John's view of the flesh. In 3:6 "flesh" suggests that human beings have two possibilities of existence: *sarx* refers to the this-worldly, human mode of existence, while *pneuma* (spirit) refers to the divine mode.[37]

There is indeed a contrast between human and divine in this verse. It is especially striking that flesh is linked with the images of natural and divine birth in both 1:13 and 3:6. In the first passage, "born of the flesh" is obviously an allusion to natural birth. And in the second passage Nicodemus asks, "How can a man be born when he is old? Can he enter a second time into his mother's womb and be born?" (3:4). Jesus' answer, "That which is born of the flesh is flesh" (3:6), could be paraphrased as follows: "What is born of human beings is flesh." This is obviously a truism; nevertheless, human birth serves as a parable of divine begetting, and the point is that "birth from above" is possible only by the activity of the Spirit (*pneuma*).[38] "A man takes on flesh and enters the kingdom of the world because his father begets him; a man can enter the kingdom of God only when he is begotten by a heavenly Father" (cf. 1 Cor. 15:50).[39] In other words, "flesh" here means human beings as they are born into this world: as such they are mortal, earthly, fleshly. While natural birth is contrasted to divine birth and flesh to spirit, flesh in and of itself is not condemned—but neither can it effect the new birth. Instead, God effects rebirth through the giving of the Spirit, which is contingent upon Jesus' ascension (3:14; 7:39).

Sarx in John 6:63

Several ideas associated with *sarx* here are very similar to those in chapter 3. (1) The statement "the Spirit gives life" paraphrases the idea of birth from above and birth from the Spirit (3:3, 5). (2) In both cases life comes through the Spirit, whose advent follows Jesus' ascension. Just as life comes through the Spirit (3:5) and the "lifting up" of the Son of man (3:14–15), so in chapter 6 the presence of the life-giving Spirit (6:63) is contingent upon the ascension of the Son of man (6:62). (3) In both instances "spirit" is linked with Jesus' teaching or words (3:12; 6:63b). (4) Finally, in neither case is human flesh capable of effecting eternal life.

But 6:63 echoes 8:15 as well. In 8:15 Jesus states that the Pharisees judge "according to the flesh" whereas he, as one sent from God, does not judge. The Pharisees' judging "according to human standards" or "as human beings do" explains their inability to accept Jesus' testimony (8:13). Similarly, in 6:63 the problem with which the evangelist deals is the problem of faith and unbelief. The flesh/spirit antithesis accounts for the offense taken by some disciples (6:61), their unbelief (6:64), and their subsequent defection (6:66). It is the Spirit, not the flesh, which enables entrance into the Kingdom; the Spirit, not the flesh, which gives life; so also faith is not the product of the flesh, but of God (6:65).

In 6:63, then, "flesh" and "Spirit" refer once again to the natural, physical capacities of human beings and to God's gift of the Spirit. To those who rely on their own faculties and trust their own judgment, Jesus' words will always remain "a hard saying." Only the one drawn by the Father (6:44, 65), the one to whom the Spirit opens Jesus' words, can come to him. Those who come to Jesus can thus be said to be "taught by God" (6:45): to them, Jesus' words are truly "spirit and life," the "words of eternal life" (6:63, 68).

Sarx in John 8:15

In 8:15 Jesus states, "You judge according to the flesh, I judge no one." In Bultmann's view, judgment *kata sarka* is equivalent to judgment by appearances (*kat' opsin*): "It is restricted in its judgment to the human sphere, and breaks down when applied to anything which puts this sphere in question."[40] Schnackenburg, on the other hand, suggests that it is a statement about the manner in which the Pharisees judge, namely, according to their fleshly natures, as those who "are from below" (8:23).[41] Similarly, Käsemann paraphrases 8:15 as "You judge as men do."[42] Verse 16 lends support to this interpretation, inasmuch as the basis for Jesus' judgment is that he was sent from the Father (cf. v. 17): his divine origin contrasts with their solely human origins.

Sarx in John 17:2

Virtually all commentators are in agreement that in 17:2 "all flesh" is a common Old Testament phrase for humanity.[43] Brown adds that "the usual Johannine dualism between flesh and spirit is not in view here."[44] But at least in several other instances (1:13–14; 8:15), John does not envision a spirit/flesh antithesis when he uses the term "flesh," although it can be said to stand over against God because it signifies that which is physical and natural.

Sarx in John 6:51c–58

Just as a large part of the discussion of Jesus' humanity in the Fourth Gospel centers on the meaning of John 1:14, and especially on the clause "the Word became flesh," so an equally important part of the discussion focuses on the bread of life discourse in John 6.[45] This is not accidental: 1:14 and 6:51–58 are the only passages in the Gospel in which *sarx* is used explicitly of Jesus.[46] In John 6, in fact, *sarx* appears more often than the sum of all its other uses in the Gospel. But the pattern is odd. Occurrences of the word *sarx* are not scattered evenly throughout the chapter: they begin only with 6:51 and are concentrated in vv. 51–58; *sarx* is used only once more, in 6:63. And therein lies the problem. Numerous scholars have contended that the meaning of *sarx* in vv. 51–58 differs radically from its meaning in 6:63 and that these verses therefore interpolate a decisively new—and later—understanding of *sarx* into the previously existing discourse.[47] If this is true and 6:51–58 does not come from the pen of the evangelist, it cannot be used as data in determining the Gospel's view of Jesus' flesh.[48]

This is Bultmann's argument.[49] Bultmann's main objection to attributing the so-called eucharistic discourse (6:51c–58) to the evangelist is that in 6:27–51b the "bread of life" refers to the Son himself, who gives life to those who believe in him. But 6:51c–58 clearly reinterprets the preceding discourse in terms of the sacramental meal of the eucharist, understood as a *pharmakon athanasias* (the medicine of immortality).[50] No longer does the Revealer give life to those who believe; rather the sacramental act provides the means by which the believer appropriates such life. Not only do vv. 51c–58 radically reinterpret the preceding discourse in terms of the eucharist, but they speak of *sarx* in a decidedly non-Johannine manner, that is, as material substance rather than as human frailty, transitoriness, and futility.[51]

Given Bultmann's definition of flesh, his judgment appears valid. "Flesh" in 6:51c cannot designate that which is illusory, inauthentic, futile, and helpless because in 6:52–58, eating this bread gives life. Bultmann's view of bread in 6:51c–58 as the "medicine of immortality," as well as his equation of "flesh" with the bread of the eucharist, lie behind his dismissal of the concept of *sarx* in this passage as alien to Johannine thought. But there are good reasons for contesting Bultmann's conclusions.

Bultmann understands "I shall give" (6:51) as a reference to the distribution of the bread in the celebration of the Lord's Supper. It thus marks the beginning of the redactor's addition, since it introduces a new idea into the discourse. But numerous commentators contend that 6:51c refers primarily to Jesus' death on the cross.[52] If indeed 6:51c is an allusion to the death of Jesus as that which "gives life to the world," then "flesh" does not refer to the "medicine of immortality" of the eucharist.[53]

In support of this reading one can adduce the parallels between it and other passages in the Gospel in which Jesus speaks of his coming death. Characteristic of these passages is the emphasis placed on Jesus' voluntary giving of his own life. This theme is repeated emphatically in the discourse about the good shepherd— "I lay down my life for the sheep," "I lay down my life," and "I lay it down of my own accord" (10:15, 17–18). Jesus' willingness and initiative in giving himself in death clearly echoes the statement in 6:51, "the bread which I shall give for the life of the world is my flesh."

Not only does 6:51 parallel other passages in the Gospel, it also elucidates two statements found earlier in chapter 6 itself: "Do not labor for the food which perishes, but for the food which endures to eternal life, which the Son of man will give to you" (6:27) and "the bread of God is that which comes down from heaven, and gives life to the world" (6:33).[54] How that life becomes available is made clear in 6:51: it is by his death that Jesus gives life to the world. When read as mutually explanatory statements, 6:27, 33, and 51 point to Jesus' death as the ultimate purpose of his incarnation. Through his death he bestows life. Similarly, in 3:13–15 the discussion with Nicodemus about the descent of the Son of man leads to discussion of his death, the purpose of which is "that whoever believes may have eternal life."[55]

Granted, the objection is not that 6:51 has no parallels in other passages in John, or even in earlier parts of chapter 6, but that it differs in requiring actual eating (of the eucharistic bread) as the condition of eternal life, rather than faith in the one who is that Bread (6:29, 35, 47). Hence, "flesh" must refer to the bread, and not figuratively to Jesus. But one can reach this conclusion only by ignoring the larger context. Although Jesus states that "the one who eats my flesh and drinks my blood has eternal life" (v. 54), that statement is immediately qualified by Jesus' promise "I will raise him up at the last day." Eternal life depends not on eating, but on Jesus, who is the Bread of Life and Life itself (6:35; 11:25) and who has the authority to grant life (5:21, 26). Jesus also speaks of abiding in him (6:56). The mutual indwelling ("He . . . abides in me and I in him") is analogous to the relationship of Jesus to the

Father: Jesus lives because of the Father, the believer lives because of Jesus—*not* because of "eating" (6:57).

While it is true that the first part of the bread of life discourse (6:36–51a) speaks explicitly of faith and believing, nevertheless, when it speaks of Jesus *as bread* it retains imagery appropriate to eating. Following Jesus' first declaration "I am the bread of life" (6:36) he states "he who comes to me shall not hunger." This is explained, but not replaced, by the language of faith in the rest of the verse. After Jesus' second pronouncement (6:48), one finds a concentration of the imagery of eating: "your fathers ate the manna" (v. 49); "this is the bread . . . that a man may eat of it" (v. 50); "if any one eats this bread" (v. 51a). But if this imagery is interpreted figuratively as referring to faith—even if secondary allusions to the eucharist are granted—then there is no reason that the language of vv. 51–59 need be construed literally.[56]

A further argument for the figurative character of the language in 6:51–59 is the striking parallel to the Samaritan woman's misunderstanding of the water which Jesus will give. Jesus' promise that "every one who drinks of this water will thirst again, but whoever drinks of the water that I shall give him will never thirst" makes no sense if taken literally, as the woman's misunderstanding makes clear. Later Jesus' very similar invitation "If any one thirst, let him come to me and drink" (7:37) clarifies the metaphor: it refers to receiving the Spirit, as 7:39 makes clear. So too "eating me" (6:57), a paraphrase for "eating my flesh" (6:53–54, 56), appears to be utterly nonsensical, and even offensive to the Jews (vv. 41, 52, 60). It makes sense, however, when interpreted as a metaphor for appropriating the benefits of Jesus' death by faith. Jesus' insistence on the necessity of his death is no less offensive than his assertion to have come from heaven; even some of his own disciples fall away (6:66).[57] But taken together, for those who believe these words about Jesus' descent and death are the "words of eternal life" (6:68).

That this discourse of Jesus results in division among his disciples accords well with the fact that it emphasizes not the "elements" themselves—as one might expect if the discourse insisted that "bread" was the "medicine of immortality"—but rather the effects

of eating or not eating.[58] Repeatedly in these verses the stress falls
upon that life which is the promised gift of Jesus and the death
which comes to those who do not eat (vv. 53–54, 57–58). Verse
58 aptly summarizes this emphasis in its contrast between eating
the manna given through Moses and the bread given through Jesus:
"the fathers ate and died; he who eats this bread will live forever."

Summary

The *sarx* of 6:51c–58 is not a reference to the bread of the Lord's
Supper construed as the "medicine of immortality." On the contrary, the term "flesh" refers to Jesus' flesh, his life, his very self,
which he will give for the life of the world. It is the "flesh" which
the Word becomes that he gives for the life of the world. The argument of chapter 6 asserts more than once that Jesus, the bread
of life, has "come down from heaven" (6:32–33, 38, 41–42, 58;
cp. 1:14) and it climaxes in the affirmation that he will give himself
in death. "The Logos becomes *sarx* in order to give this *sarx* over
to death; the Incarnation is being taken seriously."[59]

Bultmann's objection that flesh in 51c–58 has material overtones
is not incorrect; but is he correct that it never has this meaning
elsewhere in John? In 17:2, "flesh" simply means "humanity." But
humanity necessarily implies existence in a body, in flesh, as the
statement "He became flesh and dwelt among us" shows. In other
passages, "flesh" indicates what is human and as such belongs to
the sphere of the natural or material world. Thus in 1:13 and 3:6
there is a contrast between physical and spiritual birth. Birth by
"the will of the flesh" describes human, natural birth, and in that
sense is very material. So too Jesus' statement "What is born of the
flesh is flesh" refers to human birth.

It is impossible to deny that these uses of flesh include within
them the concept of "material substance." But this does not mean
that "flesh" cannot have different nuances. As Käsemann states,
while flesh is identified with what is human and earthly, the aspects
under which it appears may vary.[60] Similarly, in 1 John the author
of the Epistle speaks of the "lust of the flesh" (2:16) and the necessity to believe that "Jesus Christ has come in the flesh" (4:2).
Obviously the first instance carries a negative connotation, whereas

the second does not. Because the root meaning of flesh is humanity, creatureliness, what is natural and earthly, such variation in meaning is possible.

In its basic meaning, then, *sarx* is viewed as something which is neutral, referring simply to the flesh of humanity (1:14; 17:2). Flesh takes on a negative connotation, however, when those who are "fleshly" are not taught by God or given life by the Spirit. That is, insofar as flesh refers to what arises from what is natural and human (6:63; 8:15), it is not evil or wicked in itself.[61] But because flesh entails corporeality, it connotes "mankind in their weakness and transitoriness," what is perishable, transient, and earthbound.[62] And insofar as flesh denotes that which, because it is natural and earthbound, does not receive God's vivifying Spirit (6:63) or birth from above (1:13; 3:6), then flesh accounts for unbelief (6:63), and in that light it can scarcely be considered neutral.

INCARNATION AND FLESH IN JOHN: CONCLUSIONS

I have argued that flesh (*sarx*) in the Fourth Gospel denotes that which is human and natural (1:13; 3:6; 8:15; 17:2). Insofar as flesh rejects God's gift of the Spirit (6:63), it connotes that which stands in opposition to God (1:13; 3:6). Thus *sarx* refers to the human realm in contrast to the divine and natural existence in contrast to the life given by the Spirit. In fact the antithesis of *pneuma* and *sarx* is yet another way of expressing the Johannine antithesis between the realms above and below, between heaven and earth.[63] Descent from heaven into this world naturally entails existence in the flesh. In John 6, Jesus states that he has "come down from heaven" in order to give life to the world by giving his "flesh" (6:33, 39, 50–51, 57–58). His "descent" ("coming down from heaven") cannot be described without reference to the "flesh" which he gives.

So also in 1:14 Jesus' "flesh" and "descent" are linked, even though the language of "descent" is not used. For 1:14 asserts that the Logos who "was with God" is also the Logos who "became flesh" and "dwelt among us." That is, the one who was with God has dwelt on the earth as flesh. Just as chapter 6 speaks of Jesus' "coming down from heaven" in order to give his "flesh," so 1:14 speaks of the "Word who was with God" and subsequently "became flesh." Clearly both 1:14 and the references in chapter 6 imply that Jesus' "descent" from above or from God entailed his "enfleshment."

Although 1:14 is not an apologetic against docetists, in that verse Jesus is spoken of as "flesh" by those who are also "flesh" (17:2), and thus his likeness to them is affirmed. Only because "the Word became flesh" and because "he dwelt among us" is it possible to say "we beheld his glory." Certainly Käsemann argues correctly that the incarnation enables God's communication with his creation, for the one who has become flesh makes the Father known (1:18). But such communication, or revelation, rests on Jesus' very real enfleshment, for although *sarx* denotes the human and natural sphere, it also connotes what is material or bodily. Thus "the Word became flesh" cannot mean simply that revelation occurred in the earthly sphere or in the "realm of createdness"; rather, it must mean that such revelation (1:18) occurred through and in the "flesh" of Jesus.

John 1:14 as the Gospel's Theme

Is there any sense, then, in which 1:14 and the affirmations about Jesus' flesh elsewhere are programmatic for the Gospel, epitomizing John's theme? This question can best be answered by reviewing the nature of the apologetic apparent in both 1:1–18 and John 6. The prologue's claims can now be summarized: As the agent of God's creation of the world, the Logos has "life in himself," and, as the "true" (only) light, is *alone* the life of human beings (1:4). This Word came and dwelt in the world, but because "his own" (the Jews) received neither the testimony of the Scriptures in Moses nor the prophets (1:6–8, 15, 18), they rejected him (1:5, 10, 11). Those who truly understood Moses' testimony and believed in the Word became children of God (1:12–13). As faithful disciples they have confessed their faith: "*we* beheld his glory," and "*we* received his grace." In sum, the conflict evident in the prologue is one between those who have believed, many of whom are Jewish Christians, and those who have not. The conflict centers on Jesus' identity, and thus

the prologue accentuates the right understanding of Jesus of Nazareth: he is the Word of God made flesh. But because of the emphases that in him alone is life and that he alone makes the Father
known and, as such, displaces the revelation of Torah through
Moses, the conflict is not so much Christological as it is soteriological.[64] In short, the prologue (1:1–18) claims that God can be
known only in Jesus Christ.

In chapter 6 one encounters many of the same claims. Even more
adamantly than the prologue, this chapter insists on the exclusive
nature of Jesus' gift of life to the world. He is the bread of life, and
he is the only bread of life. Just as this bread supersedes the manna
given through Moses, so God's teaching through Jesus supersedes
that given through Moses. Thus the conflict between unbeliever
and believer again becomes evident, and it is specifically a conflict
over where and how God is to be known. There are those who
misunderstand and do not believe that Jesus has come from heaven
and that his death gives life to the world, but there are also disciples
who remain faithful because they know that Jesus has "the words
of life" (6:69). Again, the nature of the dispute is primarily soteriological: what divides believer and unbeliever is Jesus' exclusive
claim to bring God's life from above to the world below through
his death on the cross.

The Offense of the Incarnation

If there is any polemical intention underlying John's use of *sarx*,
then, it is not to be found in the aim of proving Jesus' real humanity—this is not denied—but in the declaration that this man
who "dwelt among us" is indeed God's Word and therefore the
sole source of revelation and life. To accept that claim one must
accept both that this Jesus who is flesh has come from God (1:14)
and that he gives his life (flesh) for the life of the world. And both
claims are equally offensive to the unbeliever! John 1:14 epitomizes
the Fourth Gospel's theme by summing up this assessment of Jesus'
identity which unbelief rejects. More than one commentator has
pointed out that the prologue seems intended to affirm a view of
Christ in a situation which challenges precisely that view.[65] For this
reason the prologue accentuates not an undisputed fact, the ministry

of the man Jesus, but rather the interpretation of that fact: he is the Word made flesh, the unique Son, superior to Moses.[66] In its use of the first person, 1:14 also anticipates that it is this very assessment which separates those who believe and those who reject the Word.

Clearly the evangelist's assertion that the "Word became flesh" does offend. And it offends because the one for whom these claims are made is one whose origins are known (6:42), a human being like others (6:52). But the offense arises not from the fact that God's Word became flesh. Rather, the reverse is true: that one who is flesh, who lived and died among them, claims to be the Word from heaven is the "hard saying" (6:60) which offends (6:61). What is the offense? That he who "became flesh" claims to be the one to whom God has given "authority over all flesh" (17:2), to judge and to give life (5:21–22, 26–27). Thus the Fourth Gospel's view of incarnation manifested in 1:14 does not emphasize the mere fact of Jesus' humanity. Rather, Thyen is undoubtedly correct: to know the incarnate Word, one must look at the peculiar path which he treads, which culminates in his death.[67]

Neither Bultmann's nor Käsemann's explication of the meaning of 1:14 can be accepted. Although 1:14 unashamedly affirms that the Word became flesh—a human being—it does not view that incarnation as a paradox emphasizing the "pure and simple humanity" of the Revealer (against Bultmann). But neither can one agree with Käsemann that in 1:14 flesh serves merely as the means by which God's presence is made known on earth, for both the thrust of 1:14 and the meaning of *sarx* in the Fourth Gospel refute such a view. And just as the meaning of *sarx* in John contradicts Käsemann's interpretation of the incarnation, so too it contradicts Schottroff's allegation that flesh is entirely irrelevant for John. The statements in John 6 which insist that Jesus' death is necessary for the life of the world rebut that interpretation. John does not view the flesh of Jesus as meaningless, for he does not view the realities of this world as meaningless for faith. Preeminent among such earthly realities, which are indeed significant for faith, are Jesus' signs, to which we now turn.

CHAPTER THREE

SIGNS, SEEING, AND FAITH

In all the Gospels of the New Testament, Jesus is reported to have worked miracles: he healed people, raised the dead, and fed the multitudes. The Synoptics refer to these deeds as "mighty acts," *dynameis*. By contrast, the Fourth Gospel avoids *dynameis*, preferring instead *erga* (works) and, most notably, *sēmeia* (signs). In various summary statements, the evangelist sums up Jesus' earthly ministry by stating that he "did signs" (*sēmeia*). The early response of the crowds to Jesus rests on the fact that they "saw the signs which he did" (2:23; 6:2; cp. 9:16). In 12:37 we are told that although Jesus "did many signs" not all believed in him. According to 20:30–31, Jesus "did many other signs" which are not recounted. Clearly the phrase is significant for the Gospel, and because it is used to summarize Jesus' earthly ministry it provides a clue to the Johannine perception of Jesus as one who "dwelt among us" (1:14).

For many readers of the Gospels, however, such "signs" do not point to, but rather away from, Jesus' humanity. To expand Käsemann's question, what sort of human being "walks on water and through closed doors," changes water to wine, feeds five thousand people with five loaves and two fishes, heals the sick, and raises the dead? Such "signs" do not seem to be indicative of a human being like any other, but of one distinctly different, for they apparently reveal Jesus' supernatural ability and ultimately show him to be a supernatural being.[1] Of all the features of the Johannine depiction

of Christ, it is the signs which seem to support most clearly the
characterization that he is "God going about on earth."

Thus it is not surprising that numerous questions cluster around
the meaning and function of signs in the Fourth Gospel, particularly
as they reveal the Gospel's understanding of the person of Jesus.[2]
Three clusters of questions can be highlighted as being of special
significance for this study.

1. Have recent studies insisted correctly that Jesus' signs and his
flesh are to be understood in an analogous fashion? That is, are
Jesus' signs and flesh both realities of this world which John regards
in the same manner, whether positively or negatively? And if John
rejects signs as relevant for faith or even regards them with skepticism, as many of these same commentators assert, must he also
reject Jesus' flesh as significant? And if he does, does this not have
ramifications for his view of Jesus' humanity?

That one must recognize the continuity between signs and flesh
is argued most emphatically by Luise Schottroff. She insists that for
John the signs as material realities are irrelevant for faith and precisely in this respect are to be understood similarly to Jesus' flesh.[3]
She thus endeavors to overcome what she views as internal incon-
sistencies in the approaches of both Rudolf Bultmann and Ernst
Käsemann. While Bultmann emphasizes the importance of Jesus'
flesh, he limits the role of signs, arguing that John views them as
concessions to the weakness of human faith, which ought to attain
the goal of believing without such aids.[4] Käsemann, on the other
hand, emphasizes the importance of the signs as indispensable revelations of Jesus' glory, but greatly limits the role of the flesh.[5]
Schottroff counters that any interpretation of John which fails to
recognize that signs and flesh are parallel realities of the material
world is not tenable.

Rudolf Schnackenburg agrees that in the Fourth Gospel the flesh
of Jesus should be understood on analogy with the signs, but he
contends that both have a solidly "material" aspect which receives
positive treatment from the evangelist.[6] Schnackenburg notes that
the signs' "solidly 'material' aspect" involves very definite corporeal
realities which are firmly anchored in time and space. "That they
actually took place, that they can be attested and that they are

beyond doubt is of the same decisive importance to the evangelist as their symbolic force."[7] No one denies that there are signs to be seen, but what is disputed is the precise role of their material aspect. Is their materiality an important part of faith for John? Or is it rather a stumbling block which true faith overcomes by turning away from the material nature of the phenomenon of Jesus' works and toward their symbolic force?

How this issue is settled clearly affects our assessment of John's view of Jesus' earthly existence. For if the material aspect of the sign—the fact that it is a work done within this world and witnessed as such by human beings—is viewed positively by the evangelist, then Jesus' activity of "doing signs" anchors him firmly in this world. The first question which requires attention, then, is whether Jesus' signs have a "material aspect" (Schnackenburg).

2. What is the relationship of signs to faith? In the answer to this question lies a clue to John's view of the role of the earthly Jesus and his ministry in evoking faith. And surely the role of Jesus' earthly ministry is crucial in determining the Gospel's evaluation of his humanity. What, then, is the relationship? Often that relationship is viewed primarily in negative terms. Bultmann suggested that although signs are given as concessions to human weakness, truly authentic faith believes without these crutches. Schottroff argues that true faith is faith which looks at the signs and sees the heavenly Revealer in them, but turns away from the material sign itself. And Becker emphatically denies that faith based on miracles is possible at all in John.

Each of these three scholars—Bultmann, Schottroff, and Becker—suggests that John qualifies the role he wishes signs to play in coming to understand Jesus. Consequently, they also denigrate signs as providing the requisite basis for faith. Instead, the believer must turn away from the sign to see a greater, spiritual, or otherworldly reality in or through the sign. As a result, faith turns away from the material reality of the deed itself. It is true, of course, that in John true insight or perception differs from mere physical seeing: the blind man who gains his sight (on two levels) stands in contrast to the Pharisees who have physical sight but do not really see. But does the "insight" which goes beyond "sight" negate the importance of that initial eye-witness? In what sense does true insight arise from "seeing"? By assessing John's evaluation of the relationship of signs and faith we are given further data of his view of the material realities of this world and of Jesus' place among them. 3. What do the signs reveal? Are the signs manifestations of the glory of a "god on earth" or of one "who dwelt among us" in flesh? In Bultmann's view the signs are not in themselves revelation, but merely symbolize the revelation and are ultimately dispensable. Similar is Becker's contention that true revelation occurs in Jesus' words and that the signs are therefore superfluous. But against such a devaluation of the signs tradition in John, Käsemann counters that the signs are revelation: they are both pointers to it and proofs that Jesus is God on earth. Haenchen nuances the discussion by stating that signs are not proofs (Beweise) of Jesus' identity; that evaluation of Jesus belongs to a source which the evangelist corrects in his interpretation that signs are pointers (Hinweise) to Jesus' identity.[8] But two major works (Nicol and Wilkens) on the Johannine view of signs have concluded that for John there is a real revelation in the signs. If this is so, then revelation occurs through the deeds of Jesus, the one made flesh, in this world. This appears to promote a positive assessment of Jesus' humanity in the Fourth Gospel. But exactly what role the signs play in making known the unseen God in Jesus (1:18) needs to be determined.

THE MATERIALITY OF THE SIGNS

Schnackenburg, we have noted, insists on the "solidly material aspect" of the signs, and in this insistence he is surely correct. Especially in the first half of the Gospel (chaps. 1—12), the evangelist builds his interpretation of Jesus' ministry upon the particular signs which Jesus did. This much is clear. And yet although various schemas for organizing the so-called Book of Signs (chaps. 1—12) have been suggested, no one outline commends itself as definitive, for several reasons.[9] First, there are different lists of the signs themselves, depending on whether one includes the walking on the water (6:16—21), the resurrection, or the catch of fish (chap. 21),[10] as well as disagreement about which discourses belong with these signs. Second, the evangelist's narrative method varies quite widely. Sometimes the sign is followed by an interpretative discourse (chaps. 5 and 6); sometimes parts of a discourse enclose the sign within them (chap. 9); and sometimes the two are intricately interwoven (chap. 11). Thus various units or sections in the Gospel are of different lengths and character. Finally, because the Gospel repeats its main themes again and again, it is difficult to draw hard and fast lines between sections. For example, does the second sign at Cana, the healing of the official's son (4:46–54), look back to the first sign at Cana (2:1–11) or anticipate the discourse about the hour in which the Son gives life (5:19–47)? Whatever the difficulties may be in settling on a precise outline of the Gospel, it is undeniable that sign and discourse, deed and word, belong together.

The connection of sign and discourse is easiest to see in the following instances:[11]

5:1–9	Jesus heals the man at the pool of Bethzatha	5:19–47 Jesus is the Son who has authority to grant life
6:1–15	Jesus feeds five thousand	6:26–59 Jesus is the Bread of Life
9:1–7	Jesus heals a blind man	8:12– 9:41 Jesus is Light and Life
11:1–44 Jesus raises Lazarus		11:1–44 Jesus is the Resurrection and the Life

It is not only the bare fact that Jesus did signs which becomes important. The individual signs themselves become significant in revealing who he is. Moreover, the importance of the materiality of the signs for the fourth evangelist is corroborated by the careful ways in which the evangelist presents his narratives, and particularly in those that lead to the greatest conflicts with the Jews, to establish that Jesus did indeed "do signs."

John 5: A Healing at the Pool of Bethzatha

The healing of the man at the pool of Bethzatha is introduced by the following vivid description: "In these lay a multitude of invalids, blind, lame, paralyzed. One man was there, who had been ill for thirty-eight years." In Jesus' conversation with the man, we learn of the man's helplessness (vv. 6–7). Clearly the man is incapable of helping himself; any help must come from outside, but he has not even had that (v. 7). Then the healing itself is tersely narrated: at Jesus' word, the man is cured (vv. 8–9). The discussion which ensues between "the Jews" (v. 10) and the man who was cured focuses chiefly on the identity of the healer. The evangelist sums up the scene by stating, "This was why the Jews persecuted Jesus, because he did this on the sabbath."

While the Jews never explicitly admit that Jesus had indeed healed this man, they do not seem to question it, in contrast to the Jews who witness the healing of the man born blind. But they do dispute Jesus' assertion that he did so because of his obedience to and unity with the Father, topics which are developed in the discourse which follows (5:19–47). The discourse interprets the significance of the healing, especially at the point of Jesus' identity. The controversy centers on Jesus' authority (5:30), his origins (v. 43), his claims to be authorized by God (vv. 19, 27, 30, 37) and to come from him (vv. 37, 43): these are evidently the claims disputed by the Jews in their charge that he made himself "equal to God" (5:18). In other words, what the Jews dispute with Jesus is his interpretation of the healings. But the very interpretation of the healing demands, at least from the evangelist's viewpoint, its facticity. The discourse depends on the fact that Jesus did heal the man, that he did it on the Sabbath, that the Jews "persecuted" him for it, and that he had therefore to defend his claim to work "as my Father is working," a claim which depends on the Jewish thought that God did not cease his creative activity on the Sabbath.[12] The sign provides the basis for the discourse which spells out the nature of the Son's relationship to the Father.

John 6: Feeding the Multitudes

Like 5:1–9, which paints a vivid picture of the sick man's condition, the introduction to the feeding of the five thousand (6:1–14) portrays the helplessness of the crowds and the disciples: there is a multitude of people (v. 5), the amount of money needed to feed them is excessive (v. 7), and the resources are small (v. 9). Jesus feeds the crowd, with much food left over (vv. 12–13). Again, the actual sign is told very briefly, but the evangelist includes descriptive details which accentuate its facticity. And whereas the connection between the sign and the discourse in chapter 5 has sometimes been regarded as tenuous, the connection between Jesus' feeding the crowd (6:1–14) and the bread of life discourse (6:35–58) is direct and clear: the physical feeding of the people signifies that Jesus gives and is the spiritual bread of life.

John 9: The Man Born Blind

In chapter 9's account of the healing of the man born blind, conflict arises between Jesus and the Jews, not merely about the meaning of the sign, but about its facticity as well. Again, the Sabbath healing is a point of controversy. While "the Pharisees" do not initially doubt that Jesus healed the man but deny that one who does not keep the Sabbath can be from God, the Jews later even refuse to believe that a healing had actually taken place (9:18). The man's parents are introduced to confirm that he had been born blind and that he had regained his sight (vv. 20–21); what they refuse to comment on is the identity of the one who healed him. Apparently the Jews then accept the parents' testimony, for they want to know how the miracle was accomplished. Questions about Jesus' identity persist, however, and the Jews still scorn the man's firm assertions that Jesus is from God (vv. 30–31) and works by God's authority (v. 33). Thus the narrative makes it clear that it was not the facticity of the miracle but what it revealed about the origins and authority of the one who did it which caused division (v. 16), rejection (vv. 22, 34), and unbelief (v. 41). But the narrative also takes some pains to establish the facticity of the miracle by narrating the Jews' interrogation of the man's parents and the repeated debates with the healed man. Here is a fine touch of Johannine irony: the Jews seem intent on proving to the healed man that he had in fact never been blind!

John 11: Lazarus, the Climactic Sign

The story of the raising of Lazarus in chapter 11 has provided many scholars with material for their claims that in the Fourth

Gospel Jesus does not behave according to our best human expectations: when presented with an opportunity to heal a friend, he
turns his back. Jesus delays in going to Bethany when the sisters
send for him. Only after two days (11:5), on his own initiative (v.
7) and when he is certain that Lazarus is dead (v. 11), does he set
out. Clearly the story is constructed according to the evangelist's
theological concerns. By emphasizing the delay, the evangelist expresses his conviction that Jesus was not prompted to act by human
persuasion or motives.[13] Emphasis on Jesus' delay also serves to
establish that Lazarus had indeed died: Lazarus had been buried
four days ago (v. 17); the mourners have already come to console
Mary and Martha (v. 19); each sister in turn approaches Jesus in
her grief; Mary reminds him that Lazarus is dead (v. 32); Jesus
shares in their sorrow (v. 35); the Jews question whether Jesus could
not have cured Lazarus (v. 37); and Martha protests the order to
take away the stone (v. 39). Once again the evangelist spends the
greater part of the narrative setting the scene and portraying the
various reactions of those who witnessed the raising, while the actual raising is given only brief space. At Jesus' word, Lazarus comes
forth from the tomb (vv. 43–44).

The reactions of those present confirm that Lazarus had indeed
been raised: many believe when they "had seen what he did." These
are contrasted to those "who went to the Pharisees." Those who
report Jesus' deed to the Pharisees apparently believe that Jesus
called Lazarus from the tomb even though they do not believe in
Jesus. The chief priests and Pharisees do not dispute that Jesus raised
Lazarus; in fact, they are concerned precisely because "this man
performs many signs" (v. 47). What is at issue is not whether Jesus
does signs, but what the signs reveal about his identity. Thus the
meaning of the raising of Lazarus is spelled out by the evangelist
in Jesus' dialogue with Martha: "I am the resurrection and the life"
(v. 25).

John 20:30–31: The Purpose of the Signs

In the narration of each of these episodes there is evidence that
the evangelist wishes to emphasize that what he recounts unquestionably took place. Yet only in the case of the healing of the blind

man (chap. 9) is there any hint of a denial of one of Jesus' works. Even then the Jews soon accept its facticity. Why, then, is the evangelist apparently interested in establishing the authenticity of the signs? John's narrative method corresponds to his purpose stated in 20:30–31: "Jesus did many other signs in the presence of the disciples, which are not written in this book; but these are written that you may believe that Jesus is the Christ, the Son of God, and that believing you may have life in his name." Traditionally exegetes have focused on the nuance either of the verb "believe" (in view of the textual variants) or of the statement "Jesus is the Christ, the Son of God." But John here states his purpose in writing this Gospel: of the many signs, he has written about a few in order to call forth faith. The recounting of the signs reflects not Jesus' situation, but the evangelist's: the signs are written for those "who have not seen and yet believe" (20:29). The structure of each narrative corresponds to John's expressed reason for writing: "that you may believe."[14]

Signs and Discourse

But if there is some correspondence between the method of narration and John's purpose in composing the Gospel, then surely the materiality of the miracles is crucial for the interpretation and understanding of the signs.[15] The very structure of the narrative of the raising of Lazarus (chap. 11) confirms the importance of the factuality of the miracle itself. Jesus' conversation with Martha in which he reveals himself as the resurrection and the life happens before the actual raising. On the surface, this appears to reverse the order encountered earlier in the Gospel when Jesus did "the first of his signs and manifested his glory; and his disciples believed in him" (2:11). In the account of the raising of Lazarus, however, revelation and belief precede the sign, leading some commentators to point out that the narration of the miracle is superfluous, since Martha has already confessed her faith.[16]

Yet the raising of Lazarus confirms Jesus' words to Martha. Jesus asks her two questions: "I am the resurrection and the life, he who believes in me, though he die, yet shall he live, and whoever lives and believes in me shall never die. Do you believe this?" (11:25);

and "Did I not tell you that if you would believe you would see the glory of God?" (v. 40). Twice Jesus asks Martha whether she believes; in the first case, he promises that belief will lead to resurrection and life; in the second case, he restores Lazarus to life. Clearly the evangelist does not view the raising as a superfluous afterthought, but as the confirmation that Jesus truly is "the resurrection and the life."

The discourses attached to the signs are not extraneous appendages, but grow out of the very particular reality of the signs themselves. When Jesus feeds five thousand people, he is revealed as "the bread of life"; when he opens the eyes of a blind man, he reveals himself to be the "light of the world"; and in raising Lazarus, he manifests the validity of his claim to be "resurrection and life." What is at issue in seeing signs, then, is seeing in these "solidly material" deeds who Jesus is, just as John expresses his purpose in 20:31, "these are written that you may believe that Jesus is the Christ, the Son of God." The signs point to Jesus' identity, and they do so not as ahistorical symbols, but as real deeds witnessed by real people. For this reason the evangelist reports that they were done "in the presence of his disciples" (20:30), the guarantors of the tradition distilled in the Gospel.

Jesus' signs, then, are foundational to the evangelist's distinctive view of him. And insofar as they provide this indispensable clue to Jesus' uniqueness, it is impossible to agree with Bultmann that John may well have doubted their historicity. But John's understanding of Jesus does not grow simply out of the bare fact that Jesus did signs. Rather, not only is it important to know that Jesus did signs, but it is also important to know what signs he did. Because the individual signs establish more specifically who he is (bread of life, light of the world, resurrection and life), their materiality can scarcely be considered a stumbling block to faith, or even merely irrelevant to it. John is not so much concerned with the simple fact that Jesus did signs; he is much more concerned with the particular signs that Jesus did.

Interpretations of the signs by and in Jesus' words do not render the signs superfluous (against Becker). Each discourse depends upon and grows out of a particular sign, showing that revelation in word and deed are inseparably linked. The interpretations of Jesus' identity offered in the discourses are also interpretations of his works, which the evangelist takes pains to narrate in such a way that their "solidly material aspect" is undeniable. And insofar as the evangelist constructs each discourse upon what he deems to be the meaning inherent in the sign, then the sign itself points unmistakably to Jesus' identity. Because John treats the materiality of signs, taken singly and together, as crucial to understanding Jesus, signs are not irrelevant for faith. It is to the question of how signs relate to faith that we now turn.

THE RELATION OF SIGNS AND FAITH

In delineating the role of signs in the Fourth Gospel, the precise nature of the relationship of seeing and believing in Jesus figures as one of the crucial problems. Admittedly, the data are not easy to decipher. At times the Gospel testifies to a positive relationship between Jesus' signs and the response of faith: those who see them believe in Jesus (2:11; 20:30–31). In other places, Jesus' works do not produce faith, but rather unbelief (12:36–37). And traditionally passages such as 2:23–25, 4:48, and 20:25 are understood as disparaging that sort of faith which looks to signs: such "signs-seeking" amounts to nothing other than sensationalism, an eagerness for the miraculous and spectacular, but without the necessary deeper insight or commitment of faith.

Perhaps the most common way of unravelling the difficulties has been to assign the positive estimate of signs to a signs-source in which they, as demonstrations of Jesus' divine glory, command belief, and the somewhat more cautious or even negative assessment of signs to the view of the evangelist himself (Bultmann, Haenchen, Becker, Bornkamm, and many others). Others have suggested that the evangelist conceives of "stages of faith." He does not denigrate that faith which grows out of signs, but he does view it as inadequate or provisional faith, which may become the first step towards a deeper and more mature discipleship (Brown, Schnackenburg, Barrett).

But the evidence can be read another way. In its present form, the Gospel's purpose as stated in 20:30–31 commends signs as the basis for faith: the signs were originally done and have now been written down in order to evoke faith. While this interpretation of signs in John is not current in Johannine scholarship, nevertheless, it is the most straightforward reading of the relevant texts, as the following exegetical discussion hopes to show.

Signs as the Basis for Response to Jesus

In a number of passages in John, various individuals and groups are reported as responding to Jesus on the basis of his signs (2:23–25; 3:2; 6:3; 7:31; 12:18). On the surface these passages apparently present a positive relationship between seeing Jesus' signs and believing in him. Although the Gospel offers no explicit condemnation of such a response, there are comments which suggest that the response is inadequate.

Initial response to the signs.   What are we to make of 2:23–25, which states that while "many believed in his name when they saw the signs which he did," yet "Jesus did not trust himself to them"? Apparently, 2:24–25 censures those who believed, and that censure is usually interpreted as an example of the evangelist's wary attitude toward signs and the faith which grows out of them.[17] Similarly, 6:2 reports that crowds came to Jesus because of the signs. No criticism of those crowds is offered, but their obvious failure to comprehend Jesus' words and his identity has often been taken as an indication of the evangelist's reproof of that initial response based on signs.

In these passages, however, the evangelist does not find fault with the signs nor with those who believe because they saw signs. In 2:23–25, for example, the "many" whom Jesus does not trust provide an implicit contrast to the disciples of 2:11, who believed in Jesus. One finds the same contrast between the "many [who] believed in him" and "disciples" in 8:30–32. Discipleship is an abiding commitment, whereas the initial "believing" often lacks sincerity or steadfastness (cp. 12:43).[18] But the lack of continued faithfulness cannot be attributed to faith which grows from seeing signs.

Instead, the negative judgment reflected in 2:24–25 foreshadows the Jews' ultimate rejection of their Messiah, Jesus—especially in spite of an initial enthusiastic acceptance of him—while at the same time stressing Jesus' knowledge and control of his destiny by underscoring his omniscience, as shown in his knowledge of the fickleness of the human heart.[19] One sees these elements brought together again in references to Judas throughout the Gospel. With each mention of Judas there is also a note that Judas was the one who would betray Jesus, and often, that Jesus knew that Judas would do so. The point is clear: even one of his own disciples would betray him, and yet this did not happen without Jesus' foreknowledge (6:64, 70–71; 13:11, 19) or apart from its foretelling in Scripture (13:18). Judas clearly stands in contrast to the disciples who do not fall away (6:70–71) and who do not betray Jesus (13:18).[20] In short, just as in the case of Judas' betrayal, the evangelist is careful to note that Jesus knew beforehand that such apostasy was possible (13:19) and that Judas stands in contrast to the disciples who remain faithful, so in 2:24–25 he points out that Jesus knew beforehand of the inconstancy of these Jews whose "faith" would not stand the test of time.

Again in 6:2 one finds that signs attract the crowds to Jesus. Neither a positive nor a negative judgment is rendered on that belief. And yet Schnackenburg writes that 6:2 "emphasizes" that the crowds follow Jesus not because of their true faith, but merely for the "sake of external advantage."[21] So, too, Becker maintains that 6:2 echoes the evangelist's criticism of *Wunderglaube* (faith based on the miraculous) and that 6:5 reinforces the point that the crowd comes to Jesus in "disturbing duplicity."[22] Surely, however, such interpretations read too much out of simple statements that the crowds came to Jesus because of his signs. As they stand, the verses simply explain why the crowds gathered around Jesus; any judgment on the motives for their coming is lacking.[23]

Nicodemus: inadequate response. Signs also provide the impetus for Nicodemus' coming to Jesus. Nicodemus unknowingly testifies to a true assessment of Jesus when he states, "No one can do these signs that you do, unless God is with him."[24] Of course Jesus does come from God, and this is the testimony of his works. But he is more than a teacher, for he alone has descended from God's very presence (3:13, 17; cp. 1:14, 51). Nicodemus does not err when he draws the conclusion that Jesus is a teacher who comes from God, nor is his understanding inadequate because it rests on signs. The inadequacy of his confession lies in the fact that there is a deeper truth which the signs reveal: this one whom Nicodemus calls "teacher" has descended from the very presence of God—he is "from above."

Nicodemus has not grasped the full implications of that statement, although readers of the Gospel possess a superior vantage point which enables them to surmount Nicodemus' limited understanding.[25] By means of that vantage point, the reader understands exactly the problem: it is not that Nicodemus comes, drawn by the signs; it is that he has not received the very "birth from above" of which Jesus will speak to him, that he has not been "drawn by the Father." But to be "drawn by the Father" in no way negates being "drawn" by the signs, any more than being "taught by God" circumvents hearing Jesus' words of life (6:44–45, 68). Obviously human effort does not suffice, but the evangelist does not castigate that initial faith which comes from signs nor repudiate signs themselves. Instead, he presses for the full confession to which the signs ought to compel those who see them.[26]

The signs of the Messiah.   Again in 7:31 it is said that "many of the people believed in him" because of the signs. Not surprisingly, Bultmann comments that this faith is "as little reliable as the faith in 2:23."[27] But what is really at issue here is not the evangelist's assessment of belief based on signs—he passes no judgments on the crowds—but rather whether those works reveal that Jesus is the Messiah.[28] Throughout chapter 7 there is division over Jesus' identity (7:25, 40–43). Various disputants in the discussion, including "the people of Jerusalem," the Pharisees, the crowds, and the chief priests, disagree about the significance of Jesus' works, words, and origins (7:27, 31, 40, 42, 46, 52). Interestingly, Nicodemus, who had originally been compelled to come to Jesus because of the signs, appears in this chapter to lobby for a hearing to "learn what Jesus does" (7:51). What he does, of course, are signs; and for John, signs quite clearly do reveal Jesus to be the Christ.[29]

Signs and unbelief. Later in the Gospel the chief priests and the Pharisees are unwitting spokesmen for the Johannine view of the relationship between signs and faith (11:47–48). Granted, one must use the utterances of the Jews cautiously, for in this same pericope Caiaphas ironically prophesies that Jesus would die for the nation, a prophecy which expresses the evangelist's view—but certainly not the high priest's—of Jesus' death. Nevertheless, the Jewish leaders state the problem (Jesus' signs lead to belief), albeit not without a touch of irony, inasmuch as not every one does believe in him (12:37). They themselves do not believe, as is shown in their decision to seek Jesus' death (v. 53). Just as Caiaphas ironically prophesies Jesus' death for the nation, so v. 48 ironically alludes to the future universal following of Christ.[30] Although the Jews do not understand the word *sēmeia* here in its full Johannine sense, they testify to John's belief that signs, properly understood, do lead to belief, even though the Jews themselves who utter these words do not believe. From the point of view of the Jewish leaders, the problem is that Jesus does signs and the crowds believe; from the evangelist's point of view, the problem is one with which he deals throughout his Gospel: although Jesus did many signs, the Jews did not believe.

The same problem crops up following the raising of Lazarus. At Jesus' entry into Jerusalem, "the crowd" (v. 17) bore witness to the sign and "the crowd"—presumably another group—heard he had done this sign. The Pharisees say to each other, "You can do nothing; look, the world has gone after him." In their plaintive utterance, the Pharisees again give expression to John's view that the witness of those who had seen Jesus and his signs initiated a faith which spread beyond the bounds of Judaism. Obviously the Pharisees are here, as in 11:47 and 53, exemplars of unbelief. But it is not a necessary corollary that the "crowds" manifest only a superficial faith. "Jesus' greatest act of revelation in a sign leads to a final manifestation of faith and an extreme hardening of unbelief into hatred and mortal enmity."[31]

Requests for Signs

If any passages in John are thought to reveal his negative view
of signs, it is those which state that Jesus was asked for a sign (2:18;
6:30). The following two factors are combined to yield a common
interpretation of this request for signs: (1) The demand for signs
is viewed in a negative light because John does not regard faith
which requires signs as full, genuine faith. (2) The demand for signs
parallels synoptic accounts in which asking for a sign is the demand
for a divine affirmation of one's claims through miraculous proof,
hence manifesting unbelief.[32] But these two assumptions need to
be questioned.

Nothing in the context of 2:18 or 6:30 suggests that the request
itself is evil. What is condemned is the failure to comprehend the
signs which Jesus had already done. The cleansing of the temple
reiterates the point of the changing of the water to wine that Jesus
comes as the replacement of the Jewish ritual system. Of course it
can be objected at once that the Jews were not present at the mar-
riage in Cana, did not see the sign, and hence cannot be expected
to understand its meaning or that of the temple cleansing. But in
the second instance the Gospel has just stated that the people followed Jesus because they saw signs (6:2) and wished to make him
king because of the "signs which he did." Surely they have rec-
ognized the miraculous character of the feeding. Thus their sudden
request for a sign (v. 30) appears utterly to ignore all that has gone
before.

What they do not see is that they have in fact been granted precisely that which they request. In both cases the people reveal their
ultimate misunderstanding of Jesus' miracles as revelatory of who
he is. In both instances the reader understands the irony of the
situation: Jesus had done just such a sign as the Jews requested!
For the reader, then, the Jews' request underscores their lack of
understanding. By contrast, the disciples recall the scriptural justification for Jesus' action (2:17; cp. Ps. 69:9) and eventually understand the meaning of Jesus' prophetic statement, just as they saw
Jesus' glory in the sign at Cana. Similarly, the Twelve, as representative of steadfast discipleship and in contrast to those who fall

away, understand that Jesus is indeed the "bread of life" (6:68, "You have the words of eternal life"). In sharing in this understanding, the reader also shares the narrator's perspective on the meaning of the signs.

What is criticized is not faith which requires signs, but rather the lack of faith, and that is criticized precisely because it does not understand what the signs reveal about Jesus. This leads us to question the second above mentioned assumption, that 2:18 and 6:30 reflect the synoptic hostility toward requests for signs. Typical of the request for signs in the Synoptic Gospels is the following pericope from Mark 8:11–12:

> The Pharisees came and began to argue with him, seeking from him a sign from heaven, to test him. And he sighed deeply in his spirit, and said, "Why does this generation seek a sign? Truly, I say to you, no sign shall be given to this generation."

Even harsher is the Matthean statement, "an evil and adulterous generation seeks a sign" (Matt. 16:4; Luke 11:29). Here, it should be noted, disapproval falls not on the request for a "sign" but upon the motives and character of the generation that seeks it.[33] John offers no explicit rebuke. He neither imputes motives of "testing" to Jesus' petitioners, nor—what is more important—does Jesus refuse to grant a sign. He has, in fact, already "done so many signs before them," that they are without excuse for failing to believe in him (12:37–38).

The Enumerated (Cana) Signs

John 2:1–11: Jesus changes water to wine. The two signs which are numbered in the Gospel differ in that while commentators typically cite 2:11 as an example of a positive estimation of the role of signs, by contrast 4:48–53 is thought to testify to a negative estimation of their role. But in fact, both stories bear witness to the Johannine view that signs, properly understood, lead to belief in Jesus.

Scholars generally concede that, taken at face value, 2:11 records an approbation of that kind of faith which grows out of "seeing" Jesus' miraculous deeds. But there is less agreement on whether this estimation stems from the evangelist himself. Becker, Haenchen, Fortna, Bultmann, and Schnackenburg assign all or part of the verse to the evangelist's signs-source; the more that is assigned to the signs-source, the less the verse represents the evangelist's own view of signs.[34] But the attempts to assign 2:11, in part or whole, to a source with which John is not sympathetic are puzzling. We are required to believe that John lets the verse stand as is, either without editing or with only minimal changes, and yet that in it we can still detect his negative assessment of signs. Is this not a counsel of despair? Why the evangelist does not simply eliminate 2:11 or re-shape it more drastically surely demands explanation.[35] Here we clearly have a positive evaluation of signs and the faith which grows from seeing them: signs reveal Jesus' glory to his disciples.

This last point is crucial. As several commentators have noted, the entire account of Jesus' changing water to wine at Cana (2:1–11, the first *sēmeion*) logically follows upon the accounts of the calling of the disciples in chapter 1 and the climactic promise that they shall "see greater things" (1:51).[36] It is Jesus' disciples who begin to see "greater things": they see Jesus' glory (2:11). In the signs there is a unique manifestation of Jesus' glory which leads to faith. The relationship between signs, seeing, glory and faith which is evident in 2:11 is the same as that expressed in 1:14: Jesus manifested his glory to those who had eyes to see.[37]

John 4:46–54: the healing of the official's son.   It is particularly difficult to decipher the evangelist's view of signs in the story about the healing of the official's son (4:46–54). The story runs as follows: An official comes with a request that Jesus heal his son (v. 47). Jesus apparently rebukes the man (v. 48), who takes no notice but repeats his request (v. 49). Despite the earlier rebuke, Jesus now promises that the boy will live. The boy does recover (vv. 51–52), and the official and his entire household believe (v. 53).

Despite the apparent simplicity of the narrative, there is quite a diversity in interpreting it. The spectrum of positions can be cat-alogued as follows: (1) As it stands the pericope completely denies that faith based on signs is possible.[38] (2) The pericope manifests the evangelist's reticence about faith based on signs, but does not deny that faith sometimes arises out of them.[39] (3) The unusual phrase "signs and wonders" (4:48) indicates that John criticizes an overzealousness for "wonders," for the sheerly miraculous or spectacular element in the signs.[40]

Exegetes must account for two troublesome aspects of the passage: (1) Why does Jesus initially seem to rebuke the official's request but without discernible motivation change his mind and accede to it in the end? Unlike the story of the healing of the centurion's servant in Matthew and Luke (Matt. 8:5–13; Luke 7:1–10), with which the Johannine story has affinities, there is no reference to the quality of the man's faith. It is not clear that John thinks that Jesus is moved by the man's persistence; in fact, it is difficult to account for Jesus' "motivation" at all. Just as Jesus' words (4:48) do not seem related to what the official asks, neither does the man respond to Jesus' comment about "signs and wonders," but merely repeats his request unaltered. Clearly, the present structure of the conversation is somewhat artificial, but presumably it bears the stamp of the evangelist's composition. What the evangelist has made of this story, however, is the real question.

(2) If Jesus' statement at verse 48 is a rejection of "signs and wonders" as a basis for belief, why then does the account end with the official's believing when the sign is confirmed for him? Do 4:48 and 4:53–54 contradict each other?[41]

In order to untangle the threads of this complex passage, we turn to the first question about the nature of Jesus' rebuke and the official's subsequent repetition of his request. Most helpful here is a comparison with the narrative of the first Cana sign. Not surprisingly, the accounts in 2:1–11 and 4:46–54 have several features in common. Foremost among these is the striking similarity of structure; the details may be tabulated as follows:

The First Sign at Cana	*The Second Sign at Cana*
1. Mary reports to Jesus that the host has run out of wine.	1. The official comes to Jesus with a request that his son be healed.
2. Jesus rebuffs(?) his mother.	2. Jesus rebuffs(?) the request.
3. Mary tells the servants to do whatever Jesus tells them.	3. The official renews his petition.

The First Sign at Cana	*The Second Sign at Cana*
4. Jesus' command to the servants: "Fill the jars."	4. Jesus' command to the official: "Go, your son will live."
5. The servants obey Jesus' word.	5. The man obeys Jesus' word.
6. The servants know "who had drawn the water."	6. Corroboration by the servants.
7. The disciples believe.	7. The official and his household believe.
8. Enumeration of the sign.	8. Enumeration of the sign.

Not all the details of each story are included in this comparison, but it can be seen at a glance that their structures are quite similar.[42] The similarities of structure aid us particularly in understanding the problematic statements (2:4 and 4:48) of Jesus in each narrative.

In the account of the first sign at Cana, Jesus' response to his mother (2:4) points to his sovereignty: he acts independently of all human motivation or coercion.[43] This motif occurs elsewhere in the Gospel; Jesus does not act at the urging of his brothers (7:6), nor at that of his disciples (11:6).[44] In his response to the official (4:49), Jesus makes it clear that just as his first sign was not done at human instigation, neither is this healing. His words to Mary (2:4), like those to the official, appear to be a rebuff of a request and a refusal to act; but in both cases, having distanced himself from the petitioner, he performs a sign.

Moreover, Jesus emphasizes that his works are done in his own time, his own "hour," and the use of the word "hour" marks a further similarity between the two Cana accounts. In the first instance, Jesus' explicit statement, "My hour has not yet come" (2:4) bespeaks his independence of external motivation. In 4:48–54 there is a thrice-repeated reference to the "hour" when the healing, by Jesus' word, actually occurred. Verse 53 explicitly states that the healing took place in "the hour when Jesus had said to him, 'your son will live.' " Such a statement takes on peculiar significance in light of 5:25, "Truly, truly, I say to you, the hour is coming, and now is, when the dead will hear the voice of the Son of God, and those who hear will live," and 5:28, "The hour is coming when all who are in the tombs will hear his voice, and come forth" (cp. 5:21, 24, 26). In the presence of the eschatological hour, the Son has supremacy to grant the gift of life to whom he will.

Both Cana signs show Jesus' supremacy over earthly circumstances and events. Just as Jesus does not supply wine simply to grant his mother's petition, neither does he heal simply to grant the petition of the official. John 4:48 does not rebuke the request for a sign, but rather rebukes the attempt to force Jesus to work in the hour of another instead of in his own hour. Once Jesus' independence is established, the official's repetition of his request (4:49) paves the way for Jesus' word of command (compare Mary's order to the servants at 2:5).

The second question raised by this passage is whether 4:48 actually denigrates signs-faith. If so, how is that to be squared with the conclusion of the pericope, where the official and his household appear to believe when the healing is confirmed? Haenchen correctly notes that "belief" has different meanings in vv. 50 and 53: in the first instance, the official believes that his son will live; and in the second, he believes in Jesus.[45] Moreover, Haenchen—to take one example—is also correct when he states that the man comes to true faith when the exact hour of the healing is confirmed. Therefore, it is difficult to escape the obvious conclusion that the official and his household believe because of the sign. For this reason, I find it difficult to agree that 4:48 constitutes a rebuke of believing because of signs. What is at issue, then, is precisely what brings about this "absolute faith," that is, faith in Jesus.

It is helpful here to examine, as many commentators do, a particularly prominent rabbinic parallel from *Berakoth* 34b:[46]

> Once a son of Rabban Gamaliel (II) was ill. He sent two disciples to R. Hanina b. Dosa, that he might pray for mercy for him. When he (b. Dosa) saw them, he went up into the attic and implored mercy for him. When he came down he said to them, "Go, for the fever has left him." They said to him, "Are you a prophet then?" He answered them, "I am no prophet, nor am I a prophet's son; but thus have I received tradition: When my prayer runs freely in my mouth I know that the person concerned has been accepted; but if it does not, I know that he will be carried off." They returned and noted the hour in writing. When they came back to Rabban Gamaliel he said to them,

"By the Temple service! You have said neither too little nor too much; it happened exactly so that in that hour the fever left him and he asked for water to drink."

The parallels are obvious and striking: (1) A son is healed, (2) at a distance, (3) of a fever, (4) precisely in that hour when the rabbi promised the petitioner(s) that the boy would live.

What is apparently overlooked, however, but is of crucial significance here is that when R. ben Dosa commands, "Go, for the fever has left him," the petitioners, Gamaliel's disciples, ask, "Are you a *prophet* then?" It is ben Dosa's *prophetic* word that is verified by the confirmation of the hour in which the boy improved. The rabbinic parallel illumines the Johannine pericope in two ways: (1) The official's belief in Jesus' word (v. 50) might best be understood as belief in Jesus' prophetic statement "Go, your son will live," without necessarily implying a belief that Jesus himself would heal the boy by a miracle. But when the healing is confirmed, the man apparently understands it as a confirmation not only of Jesus' prophecy, but also of the power of his word to give life. While this is not made explicit in the text, it is clear that the official does come to some sort of belief of which the evangelist approves (v. 53), that this depends on the confirmation of Jesus' words ("Your son will live"), and that immediately following this pericope in the Gospel comes another healing and the discourse about the Son's power to give life.

(2) Immediately preceding this account is the enigmatic Johannine statement "A prophet has no honor in his own country." This statement is preceded by the narrative of Jesus' encounter with the Samaritan woman in which her perception that Jesus is a prophet (4:19) becomes a confession that Jesus is the Messiah (4:29) and "Savior of the world" (4:42). Underlying the pericope of the official's son, then, is the Johannine argument that Jesus is more than a prophet. True faith does not rest content with belief in Jesus as prophet, but comes about because of the sign and, more specifically, because it is a sign of life. While not necessarily an explicit denial of the appropriateness of applying to Jesus the designation "prophet," the pericope is an affirmation of the importance of signs both for recognizing who Jesus is and, because of that function, for

their role in leading one to authentic faith. In the view of the fourth
evangelist, signs reveal Jesus' unique salvific role and are thus peculiarly able to elicit faith in him (cf. 2:11; 20:30–31). The healing
of the official's son points to Jesus as the one who gives life, for in
this healing Jesus does indeed bestow life. While signs are pointers
to the truth, they are also manifestations or demonstrations of that
truth. In this context, then, one must say that signs are works which
confirm Jesus' words (5:36; 10:37–38).

The story of the healing of the official's son can be compared
not only with the account of the changing of water to wine, but
also with the story of the appearance to Thomas. They have in
common a relationship between seeing and believing. In both accounts, belief appears to be dependent upon seeing. Jesus' words
to Thomas (20:27, 29) are often taken as a rebuke of the disciple's
lack of faith precisely because he has asked that he might see in
order to believe; his faith depends on seeing. But such faith is inadequate, as Jesus' rebuke of the request for "signs and wonders"
(4:48) has already demonstrated.

This interpretation of the Thomas narrative is problematic for
several reasons:

(1) The other disciples express their faith in the confession of the
risen Lord after they have seen him. Thomas' experience and confession are no different. Upon seeing the risen Jesus he voices his faith
in the Lord, as had the other disciples, in the Gospel's climactic
confession: "My Lord and my God!" Clearly the confession of Jesus
as Lord is a confession of which the evangelist approves and, just
as clearly, it follows upon the appearance of the risen Lord.

(2) Jesus' command to Thomas, "Do not be faithless," should
not be taken as a negative assessment of Thomas' statements in
20:25. Rather, Thomas is given a choice. Now that he has seen the
risen Jesus, he may be unbelieving (*apistos*) or believing (*pistos*).
This is basically an invitation to a full Christian confession, but it
comes only after the resurrection appearance.[47]

(3) Jesus' words "You have believed because you have seen me"
(20:29) state what has happened. One cannot read a rebuke of
Thomas into these words. Neither can one read a rebuke into the
statement "Blessed are those who have not seen and yet believe,"

for Jesus does not say they are more blessed, nor that those who believe when they see are not blessed. Instead, the structure of the narrative has confirmed that belief may follow seeing. But it also makes it clear that there are those who will believe without seeing. These are the second and subsequent generations of disciples, the readers of the Gospel.[48]

In sum, the narratives of the signs at Cana point to the positive relationship between seeing signs and believing in Jesus. Although they may well come from a distinctive tradition, as their enumeration suggests, nothing in the evangelist's handling of that tradition can be called critical of signs or of faith based on them. Instead, both signs further illumine Jesus' identity as the one who gives new life to the world.

Misunderstandings

> When the people saw the sign which he had done, they said, "This is indeed the prophet who is to come into the world!" Perceiving then that they were about to come and take him by force to make him king, Jesus withdrew again to the hills by himself. (John 6:14–15)

This reaction of the crowds is generally interpreted as revealing an inadequate response to signs. Jesus' knowledge of their apparent intentions and his subsequent withdrawal make this clear. But Jesus does not withdraw because the crowds responded to the sign. As the text clearly states, he withdraws because he knows that they wished to make him king.[49] Jesus is not "king of the Jews," if that means he is made king by their acclamation. Rather, his kingdom is not "of this world"; it is neither established nor authorized by human volition but comes solely from God (cp. 18:33–36). As Meeks summarizes, "Jesus' flight cannot imply a rejection of the term 'king' as such: it need hardly be emphasized again that for the evangelist Jesus *is* a king. What is rejected is worldly force (*harpazein*, cf. 18.37) and the world's 'hour,' which is not yet his own (cf. 7.6)."[50] In short, Jesus does not disapprove of the crowd's enthusiasm because it is an enthusiasm based on signs, but because the crowd misunderstands the ultimate meaning of the sign.[51]

If Jesus' withdrawal (6:14–15) is neither a rejection of the terms "prophet" or "king" nor a radical rejection of signs-faith, then what precisely is the nature of the crowd's misunderstanding which causes Jesus to withdraw? Here a comparison with the account of the Samaritan woman is instructive. The confession of the crowds in 6:14 parallels that of the Samaritan woman in 4:19, "Sir, I perceive that you are a prophet." In that discussion Jesus leads the woman to a higher realization: he is the promised Messiah and Savior of the world. So in chapter 6 the evangelist wishes to make the point that Jesus is not only greater than the prophet Moses, who gave the bread in the wilderness, but is himself that living bread. In each instance, the conversation begins with the recognition of Jesus as prophet. Furthermore, in each narrative there is a misunderstanding of the nature of Jesus' gift: the woman asks for "living water," thinking it will save her from coming to the well; the crowd in chapter 6 wishes to "eat their fill of the loaves." But what Jesus promises is far greater: he promises heavenly realities which offer deeper, spiritual nourishment.

John 6:14–15 presents a criticism of the misunderstanding of signs, but not necessarily of all faith which is based on them. Had the crowd truly "seen signs" (6:26), they would have understood that the feeding revealed that Jesus is the bread of life. Then they would have sought him because they saw "signs": they would have understood who he was on the basis of the signs. They did not, however, see beyond the mere material level to the meaning in the sign itself. When Jesus states, "You sought me not because you saw signs," he points to a positive link between signs, properly understood as revelations of Jesus' identity, and faith. The feeding is a sign, for it manifests, demonstrates, points to Jesus' true identity as the one "from above." Whereas the experience of the feeding should have led the people to a deeper vision, they perceived only an outward miracle and not the feeding's revelatory and christological significance.[52]

Jesus' identity as revealed by the signs is again the source of misunderstanding and dispute in the narrative of the man born blind (chap. 9). Although the evangelist explicitly notes, "There was a division among them" (9:16), Becker pushes the evidence too far when he concludes that the evangelist wishes to demonstrate the questionableness of miracles altogether by calling attention to the fact that the people could not agree about the meaning of the miracle or whether it even happened.[53] What is debated is the significance of the miracle and, more specifically, whether it indicates that Jesus has come from God in view of the apparently contradictory fact that he has broken the Sabbath by healing the blind man. John's own assessment is made clear in the confession, "If this man were not from God, he could do nothing" (9:33), and in the subsequent judgment of the Pharisees as blind and guilty (9:39–41). Those whose eyes are opened by Jesus understand that his signs attest that he indeed comes from God. For them the sign establishes that Jesus is the light of the world (cp. 1:4–5, 9) and Son of man (1:51).

Johannine Summarizing Statements

Like references to the signs elsewhere in the Gospel, John 10:41–42 states that "many believed" in him. But it is not stated explicitly that they believed in him because of the signs. Simply put, the verse acknowledges the veracity of John's testimony to Jesus, but adds that "he did no sign." What is puzzling is the relationship between the two assertions, "John did no sign," and "everything that John said about this man was true." Ernst Bammel has offered an explanation which seeks to solve this problem.[54] Bammel argues that John 10:41 reflects debate between Jews and Christians arising from the belief that a prophet's words were to be confirmed by a miracle or miracles. As was universally acknowledged, John the Baptizer was not a miracle worker.[55] Nevertheless, although he "did no sign," the Christian community maintained that his witness to Christ was truthful. Thus the relationship between the two clauses is clear: John's words remain valid as testimony to Christ even though he did no (confirming) miracle. Certainly there is an implicit contrast between John, who did no sign, and Jesus, who did many signs (12:37; 20:30). But these verses do not denigrate John; rather, they underscore the truthfulness of his witness to Jesus. And, more to the point, if this interpretation of the passage is correct, it implies a positive view of signs overall and a correspondingly positive assessment of Jesus' activity of doing signs.

If 10:41–42 refers to the "many" who believed on the basis of John's testimony, then 12:37 speaks of those who did not believe despite the testimony of the signs: "Although he had done so many signs before them, yet they did not believe in him." On the surface, this statement implies that they should have believed because of the signs. But many commentators are not willing to accept such an interpretation. Bultmann and Becker, for example, suggest that the evangelist is able to appropriate this statement from his source by subsuming its view of signs under his own belief that superior revelation is found in Jesus' word.[56] They are faced, however, with the difficulty of explaining why John accepts the statement as it is, without correcting it by adding a reference to the failure of the Jews to understand Jesus' word.

But is this verse really so strange for John? The Gospel contains more than one narrative which illustrates how a sign of Jesus leads to faith, as well as the chief example—the raising of Lazarus—of a sign which leads to unbelief. Thus the plain surface meaning of the text must be accepted: Jesus' signs should have led to belief, but in fact they did not. That the fault lies not with the signs but rather within those who rejected the signs is established by the Old Testament testimonia which speak of the "blinding" and "hardening" of unbelievers as well as by their hypocritical disposition (12:43). Barrett writes, "Signs do not suffice if God does not give men the eyes to see," and this is true of John's viewpoint.[57] Nevertheless, it is also true, as Becker points out, that the "predestinarian" tone of 12:39–40 does not excuse the Jews but rather emphasizes their guilt.[58]

Similarly, the evangelist's stated purpose—to write an account of Jesus' signs so that those who read it may believe in him—points to a positive link between signs and faith. Here again note that the evangelist explicitly states that Jesus did many signs "in the presence of the disciples." By virtue of the fact that the disciples saw signs, believed in Jesus, and passed on their faith and their traditions, the evangelist writes his Gospel for future generations.

But what is puzzling about these verses is that no miracle has been narrated since the raising of Lazarus, and yet John still appears to sum up Jesus' ministry—as he did in 12:37, where the reference is an appropriate summation of his activity up to that point—in terms of his "doing signs." This curious fact has led to considerable disagreement about whether John views other events as "signs": Schnackenburg and Brown suggest that John probably intends the resurrection appearances to be seen as signs; Fortna thinks the source viewed the resurrection itself as the greatest sign, while Dodd thinks this characterizes the evangelist's view; Becker rejects both these suggestions.[59] But even if one assumes, as do Bultmann, Becker, Fortna, and others, that 20:30–31 was originally the ending to a signs-source, such an assumption does not explain why John sums up Jesus' ministry in terms of "signs" if he himself did not think that an adequate summary. Becker's assertion that 20:30–31 must come from the source "since it is inexplicable how the evangelist can use 'signs' to sum up his Gospel" simply begs the question: John does use "signs" to sum up his Gospel![60] Whether or not John includes the resurrection appearances under the designation "signs," he uses and thus evidently accepts the statement that "Jesus did signs" as an apt synopsis of his own record of Jesus' ministry.

Summary

In the Fourth Gospel the purpose of Jesus' signs is to evoke faith. John 2:11; 12:37; and 20:30–31 make clear this connection between seeing signs and faith. Where the signs do not produce faith (9:16; 11:47–53; 12:37), the fault lies neither with the insufficiency of signs nor with the inadequacy of the faith they produce, but rather with the individuals who stubbornly refuse to see. Where the evangelist criticizes belief initially based on signs, he does so not because it was merely a hungering for spectacular miracles; rather, he criticizes those whose faith did not lead to an abiding commitment, to discipleship (cp. 2:23–25; 8:31–59). John's positive evaluation of Jesus' miracles is based on the fact that they are *more than miracles*; they are *signs*. Signs (*sēmeia*) reveal Jesus' true identity (2:11; 2:18; 6:26, 30; 7:31; 9:16) as the one sent by God, by whose power Jesus both acts and speaks.

According to the Fourth Gospel, Jesus' signs were done and recorded in order to evoke faith. Indeed, in its present form, the Gospel's explicit purpose reflects precisely this view of signs (20:30–31). And yet the significance of signs in the Fourth Gospel has been, and continues to be, interpreted in a variety of ways. The lack of consensus can be attributed in part to the tensions inherent within the texts themselves (cp. 4:48 and 4:53), and these difficulties have compelled scholars to postulate a signs-source behind the Gospel whose theology of signs the evangelist transforms (e.g. Becker, Bultmann, Fortna).

Bultmann's theological agenda has also fundamentally shaped the course of investigation of the signs in John, making it almost impossible to study the Gospel without assuming that it is better to "believe without seeing."[61] According to Bultmann, the Fourth Gospel encourages faith that rests on Jesus' word, and, perhaps more importantly, that is virtually synonymous with the "leap of faith" which the disciple must take: "Jesus refuses to give a sign in proof of his authority, such as would enable men to recognize him without risk, without committing themselves to him."[62]

But it is not only Bultmann's definition of "faith" which has exerted such influence. Indeed, is not his view of Jesus as the Revealer who is "nothing but a man" also involved in his assessment of signs-faith? If God's revelation is present in "a peculiar hiddenness," in the paradoxical incarnation of the Word made flesh, then that revelation is scarcely accessible apart from the commitment of faith. Faith cannot demand authenticating evidence and cannot believe without risk. But if revelation loses that hiddenness so that it can be seen unambiguously in the signs, then the paradox of the incarnation appears threatened as well. Instead of the Word hidden in the flesh, it would be possible to turn away from the incarnate one to the visible glory of the Word; instead of sheer humanity, one would see only divinity. In short, if one accepts the possibility of "signs-faith," then does one not also come perilously close to Käsemann's view that Jesus is nothing other than "God going about on the earth?" Precisely how the signs reveal Jesus' identity is the subject to which we now turn.

THE REVELATION IN THE SIGNS

If the Fourth Gospel asserts that one is to believe in Jesus through his signs, then it is important to ask what those signs reveal and how, if at all, those signs point to his humanity. Typically John 2:11 is construed as the epitome of John's view that the signs show forth Jesus' glory, understood as his inherent dignity, might, or divinity. Käsemann apparently implies such a definition when he writes, "The prologue in 1:14 has already summarized the content of the gospel with 'We beheld his glory.' Consistently with this, the book closes with the confession of Thomas (20:28), 'My Lord and my God.' How does all this agree with the understanding of a realistic incarnation?"[63] Elsewhere he speaks of the "divine glory of the Johannine Christ going about on earth."[64] Finally, Käsemann states that the confession "We beheld his glory" characterizes the Johannine Christology to such an extent that the "true man" of later incarnational theology is scarcely believable.[65] Thus Käsemann tends to equate "glory" with "divinity," and this equation inevitably leads to the conclusion that, because Jesus "manifested his glory" (2:11), he indeed showed himself to be "God on earth."[66]

Signs and Glory

But at this point I cannot follow Käsemann. The link between glory and signs in the Gospel can be overstated, leading to the false impression that John stresses that signs are dazzling displays of Jesus' divine power. In fact, the Gospel more often links the revelation of glory to Jesus' death than it does to the signs! Moreover, only 2:11 states explicitly that signs manifest the glory of Jesus. Elsewhere, the signs reveal God's glory (11:4, 40). Thus insofar as Jesus' signs manifest "glory," it is God's glory in Jesus (cp. 13:31–32). This corresponds to the prologue's statement "We beheld his glory," for there it is the glory "of the only Son from the Father" which is seen by the eyes of faith.

Furthermore, "glory" cannot simply be equated with "divinity." Rather, because Jesus is the one sent by God and works in obedience to and in unity with God, signs reveal God's glory in him. The signs accomplish their purpose because Jesus does not seek his own glory, (i.e. he honors God alone—5:41; 7:18; 8:50). This truth is restated in various formulations throughout the Gospel: Jesus always does the will of the Father, and for this reason his works are God's works (5:19–20, 36; 10:25, 32), and so reveal God himself. Jesus' unity with the Father results in Jesus' revelation of "many good works from the Father" (10:31). So also Jesus' words are those of the Father: he speaks "as the Father taught me" (8:28). And finally, because the Son is "in the bosom of the Father," he can make the unseen God known (1:18). Jesus is the one who does "the works which the Father has granted me to accomplish" (5:37) in contrast to the Jews, who have never "seen" the form of God and, consequently, do not know God or the one whom he has sent (5:36, 43). In short, Jesus is the one who has "shown" his disciples the Father by the very works which he does (14:8–11).[67] Jesus' "glory" clearly has the sense of a visible manifestation, yet a manifestation not of his own dignity but of the dignity of the Father who works through him.

The signs do not merely symbolize the revelation of God's glory; they embody it in visible manifestations. Thus Jesus is revealed to be the Son who gives life (4:46–54; 5:19–29) in perfect harmony with the will of God (5:19–36); the one sent by God (5:24, 37–47; 9:30–32); the bread of life (chap. 6), the light of the world (chaps. 8—9), and the resurrection and the life (chap. 11). Moreover, insofar as the signs raise the question of Jesus' origins (chaps. 5—6; 9), authority (chap. 5), and, specifically, his authority to grant life (chaps. 4—6; 11), they reveal that Jesus is sent by God and works by God's authority, and that God offers life through Jesus' signs (chaps. 4—5; 11) and death (chap. 6). God truly acts in Jesus' works; herein lies Jesus' dignity and his glory. As such, the revelation of Jesus' glory can scarcely be said to be an effacement of his humanity.

Nor can I accept the proposition of Bultmann and Becker that revelation through the Word is the dominant category for John. In the first place, it is doubtful that John consciously works with two completely separate categories of revelation in word and sign. But beyond this basic objection, it must be noted that the accounts themselves testify that signs and words are one revelatory whole. For in some accounts—the healing of the official's son, the raising of Lazarus—the sign which Jesus does actually confirms his word. And yet in still other accounts the discourses follow and elucidate the meaning of the signs (chaps. 5—6; 9). John does not make it explicit that he prefers one form of revelation to the other, or that he imagines revelation in word and sign to be clearly separable entities.

Signs and Unbelief

Because there is revelation in the signs, they ought to lead to faith; yet the relationship between signs and faith as John envisions it is subtle and complex. Clearly signs are intended to lead to faith (2:11; 12:37; 20:30), but there are statements in the Gospel which indicate that sometimes faith precedes true comprehension of the miracle (11:40). In other passages, those who do not understand the signs are judged for their stubborn refusal to believe (9:39–41; 12:37–41). What is clear is that John delineates the various responses to Jesus' signs in terms of belief and unbelief, and that one's response to the signs indicates whether one is a believer or an unbeliever.

But it is the possibility of belief and unbelief which raises the question of whether John views the signs as "proofs" of Jesus' claims. Insofar as signs lead to belief, they can be called manifestations or revelations of Jesus' identity, and one can even say that they are demonstrations or proofs. But signs do not offer unambiguous legitimation of Jesus' claims: there are those who see them who remain blind, unenlightened by what they have seen. There is no proof to those who will not see. To those who have faith, signs are demonstrations of Jesus' identity; they do legitimate who he is. Thus John can say that the signs are written so that "you may believe that Jesus is the Christ, the Son of God" (cp. 7:31). That is the Christian confession of Jesus' identity, and that is what the evangelist believes the signs reveal.

The endeavor to distinguish between the signs as proofs or legitimations, and the signs as pointers to or symbols of Jesus' identity, draws a distinction where the Gospel finds none. Käsemann is surely correct in his assertion that while all miracles are signs and pointers, they are also "proofs."[68] Of course one must also recognize, as Käsemann does, that signs are not the kind of proof that persuades all who see them. Instead, they offer assurance to believers, confirming to them Jesus' life-giving power.[69]

Käsemann, however, assumes that there is a pre-Johannine miracle tradition which views the miracles as "proofs" in the sense of unambiguous legitimation. But remnants of this tradition in the Fourth Gospel are difficult to detect. Often it is argued that such a remnant is to be located in the existence of a "signs-faith" that is merely an enthusiasm for miracle and which is condemned by the evangelist.

I have argued that there are few traces in John of this particular kind of "signs-faith" or of the evangelist's denunciation of it. Misunderstandings arise not because some people clamor merely for the spectacular; rather, they are the failure to recognize the signs of Jesus as the works of God. In two narratives (2:13–22; 6:22–34) the request for a sign has actually been granted, but those who ask for a sign have failed to comprehend that fact.

As God's attestations of Jesus, signs are not given to believers exclusively. Although they provide to the believer reassurance of Jesus' claims and identity, they also provide the answer to the question of who Jesus is and, as such, are manifestations to all. The signs answer the questions of Jesus' identity by means of specific acts: they testify to his authority (5:30); his origins (5:37, 43) and specifically that he is from God (5:19, 27, 30, 37; 9:30–31); and to the nature of Jesus' relationship to God. Jesus is the Messiah, God's Son (20:31). Nevertheless, it is only the eyes of faith that ultimately grasp Jesus' identity as manifested in the signs.

Seeing and Understanding

There is, consequently, a distinction between seeing Jesus' glory in the signs that he did and merely seeing the signs, and that is the distinction between understanding who Jesus is and merely seeing miracles; therefore, it is also the distinction between those who are disciples and those who are not. All these elements are subtly interwoven and cannot easily be torn apart. For the Fourth Gospel, seeing and understanding the signs belong with following Jesus in discipleship. Together they stand opposed to the failure to understand and thus to the subsequent failure to believe and become a disciple.

The proper role of signs, then, is to evoke faith and discipleship.

That signs do not always lead to such a commitment, however, is due not to their ambiguity as proofs but to the stubbornness and guilt of those who refuse to see. It is not "signs-faith," construed as a rather rudimentary belief in Jesus because of his miracles, which indicates human perversity. Rather, it is the refusal to believe in spite of Jesus' many signs which indicates the guilt that John condemns. One cannot, then, designate signs as concessions to human weakness, as crutches for faith, or as superfluous deeds which true faith must see through or beyond. Signs are indispensable to the revelation of God's glory in Jesus. They are concrete manifestations of God's glory in the human sphere, which John views as a primary—if not the primary—clue to Jesus' identity. The signs are not works which negate the humanity of Jesus, for John attributes them to God's power working through Jesus. Because Jesus works always and only in dependence upon God, these works are ultimately God's work. Clearly, the signs reveal Jesus' identity as the one through whom God does his mighty, life-giving works. In the Son's submission to the will of God, he shows forth God's glory in the signs which he does. But it is not the signs alone which manifest God's glory in Jesus: the Father's glorification of the Son is completed and manifested through his crucifixion and death, to which we now turn.

CHAPTER FOUR

THE DEATH
OF JESUS

THE PROBLEM OF THE DEATH OF
JESUS IN JOHN

If there is one aspect of Jesus' life which would seem to constitute proof of his true humanity, then that would surely be found in his passion and death. Jesus does not escape the final fate of all other human beings. And yet when John's passion narrative is compared with that of the other Gospels, there are telling differences amidst the ample similarities. Missing from the account is Jesus' agony in Gethsemane. At his arrest, the Roman cohort sent to seize him falls prostrate at his feet, overcome with awe. On trial before Pilate, he speaks of the divine origin of his kingdom and power, which far surpasses Pilate's. He requires no assistance in carrying his cross. Subject to no one but God, he willingly lays down his life and dies, not with a cry of dereliction on his lips, but with a triumphant "It is finished!"

In short, the Johannine passion narrative appears to obliterate the traces of suffering and agony associated with it in the other Gospels and to eschew the Pauline theology of the weakness and foolishness of the cross, thereby appearing to lessen the reality of death and the ignominy of crucifixion. Does it also, then, lessen the reality of Jesus' humanity? To state the problem another way, no one has charged the Gospels of Mark and Matthew, which picture Jesus praying in the garden "let this cup pass from me," and

crying out from the cross, "My God, my God, why has thou forsaken me?" with "naive docetism." Does the Johannine narrative,
suffused with the aura of Jesus' supreme confidence in his sovereignty over circumstances, minimize either the reality or the significance of the death of the man "Jesus of Nazareth"? Is Jesus'
death so radically reinterpreted that it has ceased to be the real
death of a real human being, and become instead the means by
which this "stranger from heaven" escapes the confines of this alien
world?

Such are the questions raised by Käsemann's characterization of
the passion narrative of the Fourth Gospel, crystallized in his statement that the account of Jesus' trial, crucifixion, and death are "a
mere postscript which had to be included because John could not
ignore this tradition nor yet could he fit it organically into his
work."[1] "The solution," writes Käsemann, "was to press the features of Christ's victory upon the passion story." In this assessment
the passion narrative does nothing to ameliorate the charge that
the Gospel is "naively docetic" but actually contributes to the picture of the Johannine Christ as "God on earth" in two ways. First,
the narrative obscures those aspects of Jesus' demeanor, motivation,
and action which might point away from a Christology of glory in
another direction. That is, one cannot explain what Jesus does and
why he does it in terms of human behavior. For example, Jesus'
death can scarcely be described as an act of human obedience, for
there is no real moral choice for one who is already and always
one with God. And neither is his death a willing humiliation, as it
is in the Christ-hymn of Philippians 2: in the Fourth Gospel Jesus
comes from glory, is characterized by glory during his entire earthly
life, and returns to that pre-existent glory. There is no movement
from humiliation to exaltation, no reversal of fortunes typical of
the Synoptic passion narratives, and hence no change in Jesus' status
effected by his death.

Second, just as Jesus' death does not effect any change in his own
status, neither does it effect any change in God's salvific or revelatory relationship to the world. Since Jesus' entire life is a revelation
of God's glory, his death reveals nothing new. Salvation depends
upon belief in Jesus and his unity with the Father, but such belief

gains nothing further from Jesus' death. If Jesus is "God on earth," present only in the "minimum costume" required for his temporary exile on this earth of which he is never truly a part, then in what sense can his death be said to be real and human, or significant precisely because it is that? Instead, it is merely the means by which this "stranger" returns to his heavenly home. In passing, Käsemann notes that John 3:16, which is often interpreted as showing God's love for the world in the death of his Son, is "a traditional primitive Christian formula" whose sole purpose in this Gospel is to stress the glory of Jesus' mission and the miracle of his incarnation.[2]

There is little in Jesus' death in John, as Käsemann interprets it, which would offer testimony to Jesus' humanity. Instead, Jesus' death is an ungainly appendage to the Gospel in which all the emphasis falls on the signs by which the glory of God shines forth. Thus there is a sharp disjuncture between Jesus' signs, ministry, and life on the one hand, and his death on the other. But what if all aspects of Jesus' life are understood by John as integral parts of his mission? Immediately the picture changes. Jesus' signs are not emphasized to the exclusion of the passion and, consequently, his miraculous deeds *and* his death on a cross are constitutive of the Johannine Christology. As a result, one might well expect that the humanity of Jesus would be of greater importance in the evangelist's theology. Not surprisingly, Bultmann's interpretation of the Gospel, with its emphasis on Jesus' humanity, views Jesus' death as the culmination of his mission on earth, whereas Käsemann's interpretation denies it that role. Thus the place of Jesus' death and the extent to which one judges that it constitutes an essential part of his ministry illumine not only the evangelist's theology, but his understanding of Jesus' human life as well.

Three Crucial Questions

Subsequent to the appearance of Käsemann's *The Testament of Jesus*, several studies were undertaken to disprove, confirm, or modify his position by analyzing either the Johannine passion narrative itself or passages which relate to the significance of Jesus' death within the Fourth Gospel. In these studies, at least three closely related questions—already suggested by the sketch of Käsemann's position—surfaced as germane: (1) What is the relationship of Jesus' death to his work and ministry? Does Jesus' death merely put an end to his revelatory signs and so allow him to return to God, or is it the climax of his mission? (2) This leads directly to the second question: Does Jesus' death effect a change in God's relationship to the world, so that it is an indispensable part of his salvific work? Does Jesus' death effect a change in his status, or is that status in fact one of pure, unchanged glory? In short, is Jesus' death an essential part of Johannine theology and Christology? (3) What is the peculiarly Johannine interpretation of Jesus' passion and death? Surely Käsemann and others correctly point out some of the distinctive features of John's passion narrative. How are these to be accounted for?

1. On the whole, the question of the relationship of Jesus' life and ministry to his death is generally resolved in favor of Bultmann. That is, one finds exegetes arguing that Jesus' death completes his mission and is thus integral to it, whether this mission is viewed primarily as one of glorifying the Father's name (Richter),[3] cleansing and convicting (Hegermann),[4] or of the revelation of God (Forestell).[5] Because the evangelist regards Jesus' death as an integral part of his mission, it is, therefore, also a part of his Gospel which cannot be dismissed as an extraneous bit of tradition.[6]

2. Just as Jesus' death is regarded as the completion of his mission, it follows that there must be some change effected by that death, whether it be a change in Jesus' status or in the relationship of God to the world. Many scholars, including Richter, Thyen, Hegermann, Forestell, Becker, and Wengst,[7] have opposed Käsemann at this point. Nevertheless, Käsemann's emphasis on the glory of Christ in the Fourth Gospel has exerted considerable influence. That the cross is Jesus' exaltation and not his humiliation is repeatedly emphasized (Richter, Hegermann, Forestell, Müller, Becker, Nicholson). Moreover, the descent/ascent schema against which Jesus' exaltation is to be understood receives considerable emphasis, as does Käsemann's thesis that death constitutes the Son's passage to the Father. On the question of whether the death of Jesus effects any change, there has been a negative reaction to Käsemann's position. And yet there remains considerable agreement that one cannot sim-

ply take over other New Testament evaluations of the meaning of Jesus' death and read them into the Fourth Gospel. John's unique emphasis on Jesus' exaltation radically reinterprets the significance of Jesus' death.

3. This leads directly to the third question: How does John reinterpret the death of Jesus? What is the unique Johannine perspective which one must uncover to understand properly his view of Jesus' death? John's perspective on Jesus' death becomes crucial, as Bornkamm asserted in his response to Käsemann's *The Testament of Jesus*,[8] and this is a point often noted and reiterated. In recent literature, the question is asked, "For what purpose does John portray Jesus' death as he does?" Some suggest that John wishes to counter Jewish polemic against the cross (Richter, Müller, Nicholson), to exhort the community to follow Jesus' example (Richter, Thyen, Wengst),[9] or to assure believers of their share in life (Becker, Wengst). The perspective of the fourth evangelist—including his retrospective interpretation and theological purpose—in presenting the passion and death provides an important clue to his overall presentation of Jesus.

These three questions about Jesus' death—its unity with the earthly ministry, its effects, and the evangelist's interpretative perspective of it—have been raised, directly or indirectly, by Käsemann's assertions about the role of Jesus' death in the Fourth Gospel. Yet Käsemann's *The Testament of Jesus* scarcely examines the passages typically cited as bearing on the evangelist's understanding at this point: the parable of the good shepherd (10:11–18), the parable of the grain of wheat (12:20–36), and the footwashing (13:1–20). Käsemann briefly discusses 10:17–18, but his discussion of this passage, which speaks of the Father's love for the Son because he lays down his life, takes little note of the meaning of "to lay down one's life." A glance at the index reveals that the situation is the same for the passion narrative itself; Käsemann includes no exegetical discussion of it. In arriving at his conclusions, although Käsemann alludes to certain key passages, he virtually ignores several crucial texts which demand close scrutiny if one is to ascertain John's understanding of the death of Jesus. An examination of these passages will aid us in evaluating Käsemann's theses about the death of Jesus in John and in reaching some conclusions, not only about their correctness but also about the testimony of Jesus' death to his humanity.

EXEGETICAL ANALYSIS OF
CRUCIAL PASSAGES

John 10:1–18: The Good Shepherd

Of particular interest in this section is 10:11–18, in which the good shepherd is twice identified by his willingness to "lay down his life" (*tithēnai tēn psychēn*). Because the phrase is used with variations (10:11, 15b, 17–18) the usages must interpret each other and, in view of the clear reference to Jesus' death and resurrection in 10:17–18, the phrase must mean "to give oneself up to death, to die."[10] That dying is "for" (*hyper*) others. More often than not, the preposition *hyper* is used in John in association with the idea of death, whether of the death of Jesus (6:51; 11:50–52; 15:13; 18:14; and perhaps 17:19), of Peter's willingness to die for Jesus (13:37–38), or of one's death for a friend (15:13). When used with any verb meaning "to die," *hyper* suggests that such a death is "for the benefit of others."[11] In the Fourth Gospel, then, *tithēnai tēn psychēn hyper* refers to the death of one person for another.[12] Here, of course, that death is the death of Jesus, the good shepherd.

Second, Jesus speaks of his death as a "command" which he received from his Father, a command which includes the resurrection as well (10:18). Elsewhere in the Gospel, Jesus states that his Father commands him what to say (12:49) and do (14:31) and that he has kept these commandments (15:10). As Brown aptly summarizes, the Father's command to Jesus relates to his entire mission, encompassing his words, his deeds, and his death and resurrection.[13] Thus it can be said that the Father's command "is eternal life" (12:50): Jesus' accomplishment of his mission means eternal life for others.

Third, within this passage there is a stress on Jesus' sovereign action: he lays down his life freely, not by force (10:18), a theme sounded in various ways throughout the Gospel (7:30, 44–46; 8:20,

59; 10:39). Jesus has the power (*exousia*) to lay down his life and to take it up again (10:18), and this power remains his own, independent from that of the human actors in the drama. Yet the Gospel emphatically affirms that Jesus' power comes from the Father (cp. 5:19): even Jesus' "own" authority to lay down his life is a charge from the Father (10:18). In short, Jesus' death happens in accordance with God's will (10:16; cp. 6:38), not as a result of human schemes. That the cross happened in accord with God's will argues for Jesus' vindication despite his execution; that Jesus dies willingly and rises again shows the inability of worldly forces to exert their final power over him who always did the will of God.

Finally, there are results which arise directly and only from Jesus' death and resurrection. To be sure, these are not in conflict with the purpose of his teaching and healing ministry, but his death and resurrection are necessary to insure the benefits of that ministry. In 10:15 and 10:17, Jesus speaks of his death; in 10:16 he speaks of his mission of gathering the "other sheep" so that there will be "one flock."[14] It is clear from the juxtaposition of these verses that the gathering of the sheep into one unified flock results from Jesus' death.[15] Moreover, Jesus is the good shepherd who has come to sacrifice his life (*psychēn*) that the sheep may have life (*zoēn*) (10:10–11).[16]

In summary, then, this passage makes clear that Jesus dies for others; that he does so, as is characteristic of his entire life, in response to the Father's command; that he does so willingly; and that from his self-surrender in death there results life and unity for those who believe.

John 12:20–36: The Grain of Wheat

Käsemann gives but cursory treatment to the saying about the grain of wheat (12:24): "Truly, truly, I say to you, unless a grain of wheat falls into the earth and dies, it remains alone; but if it dies, it bears much fruit." Coming as it does at the end of Jesus' ministry of signs and immediately prior to the events of the passion, the saying occupies a pivotal position.

Upon hearing that "some Greeks" wish to see him, Jesus announces, "The hour has come for the Son of man to be glorified"

(12:23). Up to this point in the Gospel, Jesus' hour is yet in the future (2:4; 7:30; 8:20); but after 12:23, Jesus' hour "has come" (12:23, 27; 13:1; 17:1). Jesus' final hour is the "moment that will set in motion the whole process of the death and resurrection by which the Son of Man will be glorified."[17] That hour has a two-fold character, for it is inaugurated by his arrest (7:30; 8:20), which leads to his trial and crucifixion; but it is also the hour of the Son's glorification by the Father (12:23; 17:1).[18] In 12:27–28 the dual character of the hour as the hour of death and glorification (12:23; 17:1) is best seen. Jesus' prayer "Father, save me from this hour" must refer to his imminent death, for it would make no sense for Jesus to pray for deliverance from the hour of the Father's glori-fication or of his own return to the Father.[19] Instead he prays, "Father, glorify thy name" (12:28). Jesus will not pray for deliver-ance from death, but he will pray that the Father be glorified in his death.[20] And he will not pray for deliverance because his death consummates his ministry and is the purpose for which he has come (12:27; cp. 18:11). The heavenly voice ratifies Jesus' decision by granting his prayer and by offering an accreditation of Jesus to his audience.[21] Jesus' prayer is no charade, but represents his obedient choosing of the Father's will, and the Father accepts his obedience by answering his prayer—an expression of submission to the Father.

The glorification of Jesus in death. In the response of the heavenly voice, "I have glorified it, and I will glorify it again" (12:28), the Fourth Gospel's theology of glorification through Jesus' death is expressed clearly. In Jesus' acceptance of the events set in motion by the "hour," the Father will glorify his name, even as he has glorified it through the signs and will continue to glorify it in Jesus' death.[22] Since Jesus' "hour" has now arrived, the past and future must refer to the glory which has preceded and which will follow this particular hour, the glory manifested in Jesus' signs (2:11; 11:4, 40) and death (12:23; 13:31–32; 17:1–2). In fact, verbal references (*doxazō*) are concentrated in the second half of the Gospel (chaps. 13—21). As John 12:23–29 makes clear, glorification is integrally linked to the passion of Jesus. In the vast majority of usages, the "glory" which is spoken of comes from God and is given to Jesus. It is not inherent in Jesus himself (7:18; 8:50, 54; 11:4; 17:22, 24). Only 1:14; 2:11; and 12:41 speak of "his [Jesus'] glory," and in 1:14, that glory derives from Jesus' being "the only Son from the Father." Elsewhere in the Gospel Jesus denies that he seeks his own glory (5:41; 8:50, 54) and urges others to seek God's glory (5:44). That God's glory can be actively sought and is done so only by Jesus shows that God's glory is external to him and is granted to him by God. And so it is that when Jesus' own glory is spoken of, that glory always reveals the mutual glory of Father and Son: in 11:4, "[This illness] is for the glory of God, so that the Son of God may be glorified by means of it." This is particularly true of the references to glorification which are tied to Jesus' death (12:23, 28; 13:31–32; 14:13; 16:14–15; 17:1, 4–5), in which Jesus is glorified through God's glorification of him. Jesus' glory is granted to him by the Father, the one who sent him, and thus it reflects his dependence upon the Father.

That Jesus' glory comes from God fits with the frequent use of the verb *doxazō* in the Fourth Gospel. Jesus will "be glorified" (12:23; 13:31; 16:14; cf 7:39): this denotes an action, not a static possession.[23] Moreover, it is God the Father who glorifies Jesus (13:32; 14:13; 17:1, 5), even as elsewhere the Father gives his glory to Jesus. Again, what is in view is a process, an event. But what, then, of the statements that speak of Jesus' pre-existent glory which he shared with the Father? John 17:5, for example, refers to such glory (cp. 17:24). But if Jesus possessed that glory in his pre-existent state and manifested it on earth, is there any real sense in which his "glorification" constitutes a new or different glory? That Jesus prays for God's glorification indicates that he does not yet fully possess that glory. Although John 17:5 does indeed speak of the glory Jesus had with the Father "before the world was made," that verse must be read in its context, for there are also references to the glorification which will occur in the hour (17:1) after the completion of Jesus' earthly work (17:4) and which thus lies yet in the future (17:5).

The Father's glorification of the Son, even in death, receives such prominence that one cannot deny that Käsemann correctly notes that all references to Jesus' passion are allusions to his glorification.[24] But for the fourth evangelist, the reverse holds true as well; that is, all references to Jesus' glorification include a reference to his passion. After Jesus' statement that the hour for his glorification has come (12:23), there follows the saying about the grain of wheat which dies. And following the statement about his being "lifted up" (v. 32), there is the editorial comment that Jesus was speaking of the manner of his death (v. 33). *Glorification entails death; exaltation implies the cross.* As Hoskyns and Davey write, "It is not that at the mention of death he hurries on to speak of exaltation, but that when events might lead him to speak directly of Christ's glory he obstinately refers to his death."[25] In other words, the evangelist wishes to interpret Jesus' death more than his exaltation and glorification. Furthermore, he wants to show that Jesus' death was the beginning of that hour which leads to glorification.[26]

That God's glory is revealed in Jesus' death as well as in his signs suggests that the death does not merely provide a convenient way to end Jesus' earthly ministry, but is actually the capstone of it. If, then, Jesus' death consummates his earthly ministry, 12:20–36 also testifies that, just as the good shepherd saying made clear, there are results which arise from—and only from—Jesus' death and resurrection. In the parable itself, what results from the dying grain is abundant fruit. Within the broader context, "much fruit" looks backward to the "Greeks" (12:20) and forward to "all" who are drawn to Jesus (12:32). The fruit which is borne is thus the fruit of the world-wide Gentile mission, and hints of this mission have already appeared in the Gospel (4:35–36, 42; 7:35; 10:16; 11:52).[27] Moreover, it is only through death that such fruit is borne, for there is no fruit "unless a grain of wheat falls into the earth and dies," just as the "other sheep" can be brought into the fold only if the shepherd lays down his life (10:15–17); and the scattered children of God are gathered only if Jesus dies (11:52). While there are allusions to the future Gentile mission throughout the Gospel, it is only Jesus' death which seals and secures the harvest. Again, this pericope testifies that Jesus' death both completes and enlarges his earthly ministry.

In summary, the saying about the grain of wheat in context makes clear that Jesus' "hour" is a unique time which has been anticipated throughout the Gospel and which finally arrives at the beginning of the events of "passion week." "Jesus' hour" has in view both his death and his subsequent glorification, and refers to neither exclusively. Furthermore, Jesus' hour does signal a turning point in his glorification by the Father. God's glory had been manifested in Jesus' signs and will continue to be manifested through Jesus' death. Although elsewhere in the Gospel the glory which Jesus has is said to be his own, it is clear that it is his only by virtue of the Father's granting it to him as the Son of man.[28] Finally, there are results which come from, and only from, Jesus' death and resurrection—the abundant harvest. That harvest is the gathering in of the scattered children of God: all may be drawn by Jesus' death on the cross.

John 13:1–20: The Footwashing

Käsemann slights this pericope, commenting only, "Undoubtedly John cannot conceive of love without selfless service and surrender, and 13:1 shows that Jesus' service and surrender implies death. However, this is not the characteristic Johannine manner of speaking of love."[29] On the contrary, I suggest that the interpretation of Jesus' death implicit in this pericope shares key elements with the other passages we have examined.

The opening verses (13:1–4) provide the backdrop for the footwashing. Jesus' "departure" is imminent, for "the hour" has come. As the twin references to Judas' betrayal (13:2, 11) make clear, this is the hour of Jesus' death. Jesus' death is also the hour of his "departure" out of this world to the Father from whom he had come. The hour marks a transition from this age ("this world") to the age to come and not merely a change of locale, for the hour is a temporal turning point, and "this world" and "the Father" represent qualitatively different realms of power (12:31; 14:30; 16:11, 33).[30]

Authority and identity. Conscious of his imminent departure, as well as of his authority and origin, Jesus approaches his death with the final victory assured.[31] One finds the motif that "all things" have been entrusted to Jesus not only here (13:3), but throughout the Gospel: "all things were made through him" (1:3); "the Father loves the Son, and has given all things into his hands" (3:35); "the Father loves the Son, and shows him all that he himself is doing" (5:20); "all that the Father gives me will come to me" (6:37); "this is the will of him who sent me, that I should lose nothing of all that he has given me, but raise it up at the last day" (6:39; cp. 10:29; 12:32; 15:15; 16:15; 17:10). Because of the scope and variety of these references, it is clear that in the Fourth Gospel the "all things" entrusted to Jesus and accomplished through him refers to the totality of his mission, including his words (15:15); his granting of salvation to be consummated in the last day (6:37, 39; 10:29; 12:32); and, in view of 13:3, his death on the cross.[32] In compressed form, then, 13:3 reveals that Jesus' death on the cross is his own deed ("into his hands"), but also the Father's will.[33] Jesus' death thus expresses his sovereignty[34] as well as his acceptance of "all things" that the Father has given to him.

At this critical juncture, Jesus washes the disciples' feet, an act which prefigures and interprets his death on the cross, as becomes evident in 13:7, when Jesus tells Peter, "Afterward you will understand." Jesus' statement refers to the understanding that Peter and the disciples will be granted after Jesus' resurrection and ascension and the subsequent gift of the Holy Spirit as part of the Spirit's teaching (cp. 2:22; 7:39; 12:16; 13:19; 14:26, 29; 15:26; 16:13). That understanding comes after Jesus' death and includes the proper interpretation of that death.[35]

A proper interpretation of Jesus' death includes the understanding of who he is. Thus Jesus states (13:19), "I tell you this now, before it takes place, that when it does take place you may believe that I am he."[36] John 13:18–19 is strikingly similar to Jesus' statement "When you have lifted up the Son of man, then you will know that I am he" (8:28). So also when Judas hands over Jesus, the disciples will believe that "I am he" (13:18–19). Jesus' death sharpens the revelation of his identity, here stated in the strongest possible terms in the absolute *egō eimi*.[37]

An act of love.   Jesus' death is an act of love "for his own" (13:1).

This love is manifested on the cross, for the statement that he loved them until the end (*eis telos*) already has in view Jesus' declaration from the cross, "It is finished" (*tetelestai*; 19:30).[38] One finds the same theme in John 3:14–16. Verses 14–15 and v. 16 are parallel, for each promises the same result: both the lifting up of the Son of man and God's "giving" his only Son confer eternal life. Jesus' "lifting up" implies his crucifixion (8:28; 12:33); "he gave" (3:16) should similarly be construed as a reference to the cross. But if this is so, then Jesus' death is a manifestation of God's love for the world, even as it is a manifestation of Jesus' love for his own (13:1). Jesus' love is revealed not only in the cross ("he loved them to the end") but also in his past actions ("having loved his own"). His entire life discloses his love for his own, a love which is manifested supremely on the cross. It is, therefore, not surprising that this section which centers on Jesus' death (chap. 13) opens and closes with an emphasis on love: 13:1 underscores Jesus' love "for his own," just as 13:34–35 highlights the love which the disciples are to manifest.

Jesus' cleansing death.   In the dialogue between Peter and Jesus (13:6–10), we find yet another clue to comprehending the meaning of Jesus' deed. Peter first protests Jesus' intention to wash his feet (13:6) because it is a puzzling role reversal that one who is properly "Lord" and "Teacher" (13:6, 9, 13–14) should wash the feet of a disciple and servant (13:16).[39] Jesus replies that Peter will understand the significance of this act at a later time. Peter renews his protest: the Lord shall never perform for him the service of a servant or pupil. Jesus' second response shows the necessity of the act: "If I do not wash you, you have no part in me."

With this response several points about the footwashing and, therefore, about Jesus' death are established. First, Jesus makes it plain that despite human resistance to his death, it must take place. One who does not accept the cross stands in danger of overlooking God's chosen path for the one whom he has sent.[40] Here, then, we see an attempt to overcome objections to the crucifixion of God's anointed one. Second, Jesus' response shows that Peter cannot participate in the benefits of Jesus' passion unless he is washed—unless

he submits in faith to God's way of salvation. One finds a similar
struggle between human perception and God's purpose in chapter
6, where Jesus insists that "unless you eat the flesh of the Son of
man and drink his blood, you have no life in you" (6:53). Here
washing refers to that death apart from which there is no "part"
(*meros*) in Jesus. *Meros* (part, portion, lot), like the term "life" (*zoē*)
in 6:53 (cp. 6:51), refers to the eschatological reward of an eternal
heritage with Jesus, and is paralleled by other promised rewards of
sharing Jesus' life (14:19), his glory (17:22, 24), and being where
he is (12:26; 14:3; 17:24).[41]

But Peter misunderstands Jesus and asks for a more complete
washing, apparently assuming that where some washing is bene-
ficial, unlimited washing would be even more so. Jesus, however,
assures him that one washing is enough and will make him "entirely
clean" (13:10).[42] Jesus' reply to Peter discloses, first of all, the
efficacy of the washing, that is, the efficacy of Jesus' death in cleansing his disciples. The cleansing is not specifically explicated as a
cleansing from sin. Nevertheless, from the context one can determine that those who are clean stand in contrast to the one who
betrays Jesus. Those who are clean are not morally perfect, but are
faithful in their allegiance to the Lord. Similarly, in 15:2–3, the
branches which "abide" in Jesus are said to be "clean." To be clean,
then, implies faithful discipleship, a continued and committed abiding in Jesus by virtue of which one bears fruit and so receives a
place (*meros*) among the people of God (cp. 11:52).[43]

Not only does Jesus' death cleanse efficaciously, it does so
uniquely. The cleansing which Jesus' death effects need not be repeated and, in fact, it cannot be. It is a once-for-all event whose
arrival is signaled by the arrival of the crucial "hour" and whose
efficacy depends ultimately on Jesus' departure to his Father (13:1,
3). It is the necessary event which consummates Jesus' ministry
among his own. That Jesus washes the disciples' feet at this point
means that they still need to be cleansed, even after his teaching
and healing ministry among them. His death on the cross is the one
thing yet necessary to insure their complete cleansing and final salvation.[44] Thus his death completes, and does not merely duplicate,
what is accomplished during his ministry.

A second interpretation? This brings us to the so-called second interpretation of the footwashing (13:12–17). The first interpretation (13:6–11) emphasizes that Jesus' death on the cross constitutes a salvific cleansing of the disciples. But this so-called second interpretation shifts the focus from what Jesus' death accomplishes to that which is required of the disciples by way of response. More than one scholar has suggested that the two interpretations of the footwashing are so different that one must assign them to two different hands.[45] Jürgen Becker, for instance, states that the two interpretations are not at all related and are, in fact, mutually exclusive; for while the first (vv. 6–10a) treats the footwashing as an act which is a soteriological sign, the second (vv. 12–15) views it as an act which is to be imitated.[46]

But it is doubtful whether such a sharp disjuncture within the text can actually be substantiated. First, there are not really two "interpretations" of the footwashing, but only the one offered in vv. 12–17. Before that we have the evangelist's editorial comments (13:1–4) and the event itself, with the accompanying dialogue between Jesus and Peter (vv. 5–10), but whether either of these constitutes an "interpretation" of that event seems doubtful. Instead, we have an act which, in its wider context, prefigures Jesus' death; and this act, taken together with the following interpretation (vv. 12–17), must be read as a unit to discern adequately the meaning of this whole scene within the Fourth Gospel. At the very least, the context itself suggests that the interpretation of the footwashing offered in vv. 12–20 cannot be severed from its moorings in the death of Jesus.[47]

Second, Jesus' interpretation of the footwashing does not radically shift the focus from soteriology (a view of salvation) to parenesis (instruction or exhortation). In the conversation with Peter, it becomes apparent that he objects that Jesus, the Lord, intends to wash his feet. This is, however, precisely what is required: "If I do not wash you, you have no part in me" (13:8). Because the promised eschatological reward is participation in Jesus, he himself must perform this act of cleansing. And it is the theme of the necessity of Jesus' action which forms the leitmotif of the interpretation in vv. 12–20, for the first question which Jesus asks is "Do you know what I have done to you?" The death, prefigured by the footwashing, is Jesus' act (cp. v. 3) on behalf of his disciples (*hymin*). Jesus continues to stress the importance, above all, not of the disciples' action, but of his own deed: "If I, your Lord and teacher, have washed your feet . . ."; "I have given you an example, that you should do as I do"; and "I know whom I have chosen" (cp. 13:11). Emphasis on Jesus' deed comes to its climax in the "I am" statement of 13:19, which points towards the revelation of Jesus' identity on the cross (8:28). In short, both the interpretation of the footwashing and the event itself stress the importance of Jesus' fulfillment of salvation through the cross (19:30).

Nevertheless, in the interpretation of the footwashing there are explicit commands to the disciples to do for another what Jesus has done for them. Certainly there is an exemplary note introduced here. But obedience to Jesus' commands does not take the place of participation in his salvific cleansing. Rather, the disciples assume their place (*meros*) among the people of God by participation in Jesus' death "on their behalf." As Bultmann writes, Jesus' death is not the pattern to which the disciples must conform in order to receive eternal life. Rather, they are committed by reason of what they have received: "even as (*kathōs*) I have done for you" (*hymin*) (13:15).[48]

Barrett offers a helpful description of the footwashing and its attendant interpretation: In the Fourth Gospel, the death of Jesus is at once *salutary* (or "salvific"), for it cleanses the disciples for a faithful and abiding commitment; it is *revelatory*, for in his death Jesus reveals God's love (13:1; 3:15, 16), his identity (13:19; 8:28), and the fulfillment of God's plan (13:1; 19:30); and it is *exemplary*, for Jesus' cross provides an example of obedience to God and service to those whom he loves that the disciples are to emulate precisely because Jesus has died for them.[49]

Summary

These three passages (10:10–18; 12:20–36; 13:1–20) share elements which, taken together, suggest an understanding of the meaning of the death of Jesus which stands in sharp contrast to that delineated by Käsemann in *The Testament of Jesus*. These texts demonstrate that Jesus' death can scarcely be relegated to a remnant of tradition which the evangelist was unable to appropriate satisfactorily.

In particular, Käsemann's contention that the death of Jesus can be equated with his return to the Father, thus merely ending his sojourn on this earth, cannot be sustained. Quite the contrary, the death of Jesus is an integral part of his salvific mission! It yields "much fruit"—the universal drawing of "all" peoples, their subsequent unity, the pledge of eternal life, and the complete cleansing of the disciples. Indeed, because Jesus' death consummates his earthly ministry (19:30), Jesus can even say, "For this hour I have come" (12:27). Although the benefits of Jesus' ministry and death can be viewed as identical (cp. e.g. 13:10; 15:3), nevertheless Jesus' death is necessary to insure those benefits (13:8).[50]

In the statement "For this hour I have come," Jesus declares that his death is the ultimate purpose of his coming, the final outcome of his constant obedience to the Father. His life and death can also be characterized as service for others, arising out of love, as the footwashing graphically depicts. Because his death is a service of love, it becomes an example for those who would be with him to follow and, more important, it enables them to follow it because it cleanses them for faithful commitment expressed in loving one another after Jesus departs from them (Thyen, Wengst). Thus it is doubtful whether John completely subsumes love and obedience under the rubric of a "unity" emptied of any moral component (against Käsemann, Lattke).

Jesus' death does effect change: in Jesus' own status, in God's relationship to the world, and among the disciples. First, in regard to Jesus' own status, Jesus' hour, a unique one-time event (Wengst), initiates his glorification by the Father. Thereby the cross becomes the visible symbol of Jesus' glorification and exaltation (Forestell). Jesus returns to the Father, whose glory he shared "before the world was made" (17:5), but only after he has accomplished God's work on earth through the ongoing process of glorifying God's name. The Father's glorification of the Son is a process that is completed on the cross (19:30) and in his return to the Father (17:4–5, 24).

God's relationship to the world also changes as a consequence of Jesus' death. Although Käsemann focuses on John 17, he simply glosses over the full range of references to the "world" in that chapter and elsewhere in John.[51] The world is only the alien realm in which Jesus and his disciples dwell temporarily. With respect to 17:23, for example, Käsemann comments only on the expression "that they may be perfected into unity," and not on the subsequent phrase "that the world may know that thou hast loved them."[52] He emphasizes statements such as "They are not of this world, even as I am not of the world" (17:16) at the expense of other statements which envision a mission to the world (17:18, 21, 23).

Yet Jesus' death does have undeniable benefits for the world. It brings life to the world (10:10; 12:24, 50; cp. 3:15–16; 5:21, 25–29; 6:51, 53–54, 57–58). It ensures the universal extension and scope of Jesus' mission (11:50, 52; 12:32); and it changes the disciples, providing the foundation for unity, faithful abiding, and mutual love (12:26; 13:15–17, 34–35; 15:3–4, 8–13) (so Thyen, Wengst). Chapter 21 illustrates the point, for Peter is to express his love for Jesus by tending the sheep, which would lead finally to his death by which he would "glorify God" (21:19), and so "follow" Jesus (21:19). Peter's restoration from one who denied Jesus to a faithful follower shows that his cleansing is completed and that his faithfulness (love) for Jesus must be expressed as service to the sheep. So Jesus' death changes the disciples, enabling them truly to "follow me" (12:26; 20:19).

In short, it is quite clear that the evangelist did "fit [Jesus' death] organically into his work." This reality raises serious questions against Käsemann's claim that a thorough integration of Jesus' death into the Fourth Gospel and its Christology was precluded by John's "naive docetism."[53] Indeed, inasmuch as Jesus' death constitutes the culmination of his work done out of love for others and in obedience to the Father, John surely escapes the charge of Docetism as Käsemann defines it. For here there is the human motivation of love, obedience, and submission to God. Yet when one comes to the passion narrative itself, that human motivation appears radically reinterpreted. Unquestionably the passion narrative of John's Gospel manifests unique features—features which at first glance point not to Jesus the man, suffering and dying a human death, but to Jesus the king, who without a struggle triumphs over earthly circumstances, commanding awe and fear from soldiers and authorities. Unquestionably Käsemann is correct that John "presses features of Christ's victory upon the passion." But John's interpretation of the passion in such a manner does not stem from his "naive docetism" or from the inability to integrate it into his Gospel. Instead, it arises from the need to remind his readers of the Spirit's witness that even and especially here one sees the hand of God active. At this point, then, an examination of the pertinent passages and themes within the passion narrative is in order.

THE PASSION NARRATIVE

What follows is a brief review of certain passages and themes which are taken either as supporting an overtly anti-docetic polemic (e.g. 19:34) or as buttressing the charge that the narrative points "in the direction of a gnosticizing Christianity."[54] Of particular interest is Pilate's presentation of Jesus with the teasing and enigmatic statement, "Behold the man!" (19:5). It raises the question of its relationship to Pilate's second pronouncement, "Behold your king!" (19:15), and to the theme of kingship which runs throughout the trial narrative and, for that matter, the Gospel (cp. 6:15). In addition, the crucifixion scene itself contains two passages of note. As already indicated, Jesus' dying words contrast rather sharply with those recorded in Matthew and Mark, thus raising the question of John's reinterpretation of that death in a docetic direction, or at least in a direction which mitigates its agony and suffering—and hence its reality and humanity. By contrast, the report about the piercing of Jesus' side (19:34) has been taken as stressing the reality of Jesus' death and humanity against those who denied both. A look at crucial passages in the passion narrative can serve as the basis for corroborating John's interpretation of Jesus' death and the implications for his understanding of Jesus' humanity.

John 18:1—19:16: The Arrest and Trial

Throughout the narrative Jesus' sovereignty and victory over his opponents loom large. When the Roman cohort comes to the garden and asks for Jesus of Nazareth, his response quite clearly is more than simple self-identification. The soldiers fall to the ground in awe at the majestic "*ego eimi*" (18:6). Jesus has the upper hand here and remains in control. Although the soldiers take Jesus captive, they do so only by his willing submission. In fact, he virtually guides their actions, twice identifying himself as the object of their search (18:5, 8), directing that the disciples be released (18:8), and commanding Peter to permit his arrest (18:11). Although such stoic behavior in the face of death may be unusual, it is certainly by no means without parallel—one is reminded of Ignatius' quest for martyrdom.[55] At any rate, the issue is not whether Jesus acts as one might expect other human beings to behave in a similar situation. The issue is how these features of victory and sovereignty in the narrative express the Gospel's interpretation of that event.

Here one should note that Jesus' triumph is only one panel of a tapestry. Another panel reveals that Jesus' arrest and imminent death are the will of God for him. Repeatedly the passion narrative declares that what has happened fulfills God's word in Scripture (18:9, 32; 19:23, 28, 36, 37). Pilate acts not by the authority of Rome but by the authority of God (19:11). Moreover Jesus' dying words, "It is finished!" make it clear that his death on the cross consummates God's work in him (12:27; 13:1). Jesus submits to his captors and so to his death in obedience to the Father's will (cp. 10:18). Thus he tells Pilate that if his was an earthly kingship, based on human authority and values, then his servants would fight to prevent his death; but God's path for him includes the cross (10:18; 11:51–52; 13:8). Jesus' victory and kingship are assured precisely because he obeys the will of God completely and until the end (13:1; 19:30).

Indeed, in John there is no royal victory and no kingship at all without death. In chapter 6 the crowd's clamorous recognition of Jesus as king (6:14–15) dissipates into unbelief and leads to desertion when he insists that his mission culminates in his death on the cross. Furthermore, in chapter 6 Jesus' claims to be the "bread of life" and "bread of heaven" are set against the objection that he is "Jesus of Nazareth." Not only is the rightful King of the Jews this man of Nazareth, but it is precisely as king that he must suffer death. So also in the trial narrative Pilate presents Jesus with the two-fold "Behold the man!" and "Behold your king!"

Clearly these two declarations are parallel. But their meaning is less clear. Is Pilate's first statement, "Behold, the man!" designed to arouse pity and compassion for Jesus, the harmless caricature of a king?[56] Or is "the Man" itself a throne name, a title of honor and dignity?[57] In making a decision, one should note the frequent, sometimes sarcastic and disparaging, sometimes innocent, but usually ironic references to Jesus as "this man" (cp. 4:29, "a man"; 5:12, "the man"; 10:33, "you, being a man"; 11:47, "this man"). The designation of Jesus in this way occurs in the dramatic dialogue of chapter 9. It is "the man called Jesus" who healed the blind man (9:11), "this man" who is called a sinner (9:16, 24), "this man" whose origins are unknown (9:29) or who comes from God (9:33). During Jesus' trial the servant asks Peter whether he is not one of "this man's" disciples (18:27), and Pilate asks the Jews what charge they bring against "this man" (18:29). As Culpepper writes, "When Jesus is called simply 'a man' the implied author winks at the reader."[58] In the statement of the man at the pool of Bethzatha, "I have no man to put me into the pool," the double-edged character of the term *anthrōpos* is clear. Jesus is the man who will help him, but of course his action will subsequently lead to the charge that Jesus "made himself equal with God" (5:18; cp. 10:33; 19:7). "The man" who helps is not merely a man.

Pilate's declaration "Behold the man!" (19:5) brings this theme to its climax. Whether or not Jesus is the King of the Jews, the meaning of that kingship and its relationship to Caesar's rule are the recurring themes of conversation between Jesus and Pilate on the one hand, and Pilate and the Jews on the other. Immediately preceding the scourging of Jesus, Pilate asks the Jews whether they want him to release the "King of the Jews" (18:39). Throughout the narrative, in fact, he obstinately uses this title (18:33, 37, 39; 19:14–15, 19); but the Jews refuse to ascribe it to Jesus except as a false claim. Beaten and arrayed with royal robes and a crown of thorns, Jesus is presented by Pilate to the crowds. In the context of this scene, which so stresses Jesus' kingship, Pilate's statement must mean "Look at him! This is the King you want crucified!"[59] Although Pilate's intention may be to ridicule the Jews' charges against Jesus and so to secure his release, the evangelist intends a deeper significance.[60] And the parallelism between Pilate's two pronouncements suggests that the deeper significance is to be found in the secret that this man is indeed King. Pilate refuses to change the *titulus*, "Jesus of Nazareth, King of the Jews"; but the chief priests would prefer that it read, "This man said, "I am King of the Jews." If anything, their suggested change brings yet more guilt upon them, for it lays bare the refusal to believe that "Jesus of Nazareth" is "the King of the Jews" (cp. 6:41–42). Jesus is still merely "this man."

It is doubtful, then, that 19:5 should be attributed to John's overtly anti-docetic stance; but in concert with 19:14 it emphasizes in the strongest possible way that the King of the Jews is a human being, Jesus of Nazareth.[61] Bultmann aptly summarizes the point: the "entire paradox of the claim of Jesus" is asserted in 19:5, "In very truth, such a man it is who asserts that he is the king of truth! The declaration *ho logos sarx egeneto* has become visible in its extremest consequences."[62] That this man is king, and that to and in his death he obeys the will of God and so is the victor, are assertions which deflect any claim that the Johannine passion minimizes the true humanity of Jesus.

John 19:17–37: The Crucifixion

Jesus' statement from the cross "It is finished!" (19:30) looks back to 13:1, which introduces the events of Jesus' death by stating that Jesus loved his own "to the end." A translation such as "It is achieved, it is accomplished," referring to the consummation of the mission and work which God had given him to do, accurately captures the essence of *tetelestai*. Throughout the Gospel Jesus states that he does the work of the Father (e.g. 5:36; 10:25, 31; 14:11). Anticipating his death, Jesus states that he has accomplished the work God gave him to do (17:4). On the cross, that work is brought to its goal (*telos*), and so Jesus declares that work finished. In comparison to Jesus' words as reported in Matthew and Mark, the last words of the Johannine Jesus appear to be a statement of victory. However, in view of the likely independence of John from the Syn-

optics, it would be rash to state that John substitutes a pronouncement of triumph for a cry of dereliction, or to interpret John's words
in light of the synoptic record.[63] When interpreted on their own
and in the context of Johannine theology, Jesus' words are the ultimate, that is the last and the climactic, statement of his submissive
obedience to God.[64] Rather than suggesting the death of one untouched by human suffering, his words point to the death of one
obedient to God's command for him. "If 'it is finished' is a victory
cry, the victory it heralds is that of obediently fulfilling the Father's
will."[65]

The pericope concerning the piercing of Jesus' side (19:34–35)
is often taken as evidence of John's anti-docetic interest when it is
understood as a a testimony establishing the death, and hence humanity, of Jesus. The soldier's act can only be taken as a test to see
if Jesus has indeed died.[66] When the soldiers come to break the legs
of the three victims to hasten death, they clearly expect to break
the legs of all three; they expect Jesus also to be alive. The lance
thrust into Jesus' side lays to rest any doubts regarding his early
death.

The testimony of 19:35 confirms the undeniable reality of what
has been seen. But does the witness testify to the piercing of Jesus'
side and his death, or to the fact that water and blood came out
from his side as a result—or are the two inseparable? The answer
here depends on whether the flow of blood and water should be
taken as an event characteristic of any normal death, or whether
it is viewed as a miraculous occurrence. Bultmann and Haenchen
assert that for John the event is a miraculous occurrence, but the
view that the evangelist understood the event as a natural phenomenon also has much support.[67] Such an interpretation has the advantage that the narrative itself does not give any hint that the event
was miraculous.[68] Furthermore, it links the soldier's actions (he
expects Jesus to be alive but finds him dead) with the testimony of
the eye-witness (he testifies to Jesus' death). Theories about additions or reinterpretations of the event by the ecclesiastical redactor
are thus rendered superfluous.[69]

Thus the water and blood which flowed from Jesus' side are to
be taken as evidence of his death. But does the event have a symbolic

meaning as well? Scholars have long argued that it does indeed have a deeper significance, and what that significance is has been thoroughly debated.[70] The most plausible suggestions, which interpret the symbolism in the context of the Gospel, are that the water symbolizes the fulfillment of Jesus' promise of the giving of the Spirit, elsewhere in the Gospel called "living water" (7:38–39), and that the blood refers to the cleansing death of Jesus, the Paschal Lamb (1:29; 6:51–59). Earlier in the Gospel, when Jesus promises the Spirit, the evangelist comments that the Spirit was given when Jesus was glorified, or upon his death and return to the Father; hence, the giving of the Spirit is dependent upon and subsequent to Jesus' death. And the blood of Jesus' death is requisite for salvation (6:51–59). Thus the context of the Gospel's use of the symbolism of water and blood is Jesus' death. This further strengthens the case that 19:34 and 19:35–37 are a double testimony to the real death of Jesus, upon which depend the gift of the Spirit and the cleansing from sin. Although the pericope does not have an explicitly anti-docetic aim, it does establish the certainty of Jesus' death and the benefits of salvation which depend upon it. As Barrett writes, John was concerned to emphasize "that the real death of Jesus was the real life of men."[71]

Summary

The passion narrative does not minimize the humanity of Jesus. The themes of victory and triumph point to the consummation of the work of God through the obedience and actions of Jesus, and so are indirect testimony to the humanity of the victor. Direct testimony to Jesus' humanity is found in the statements of Pilate and in the account of Jesus' death. Neither of these passages endeavors to prove Jesus' humanity; that is assumed. Indeed, is it not precisely the problem? For the question which the Gospel addresses is who this man Jesus is. The passion narrative does seek to establish Jesus' ultimate identity (19:5, 14) and that the eschatological blessings of salvation are present in this man (19:30, 34–35). Jesus, the man of Nazareth who unquestionably died on a Roman cross, is King of the Jews, who offers cleansing and the promised Holy Spirit to the world. The meaning of his death, no less than that of his origins and signs, demands the answer of faith. Without faith one sees only a dead man on a cross, not the King who brings life to the world.

THE JOHANNINE INTERPRETATION
OF JESUS' DEATH

Undoubtedly those features which we associate with the passion and death of Jesus in the Synoptic Gospels and Paul do not figure prominently in John. But that does not necessarily mean that John's Christology can be described as a "pure exaltation Christology" (Hegermann), quite apart from the question whether such a formulation is at all helpful. Do not Käsemann and others too quickly assume that the opposite of a "Christology of humiliation" is a "Christology of glory"? Whatever the precise nuance of "glory" (*doxa*) in the Fourth Gospel, it is certainly revelatory glory (1:14; 2:11; 11:4, 40), as Käsemann himself so adamantly asserts in his analysis of the incarnation and the signs. But there is no revelation in John apart from Jesus' death! Only with the death and resurrection of Jesus is the proper understanding of these events offered to the community of faith (2:22; 7:39; 12:16, 33; 13:13, 19). Even John's narrative points to the centrality of Jesus' death by continually foreshadowing that death (1:29; 2:4, 22; etc.) and by asserting that Jesus' death is that event in which his work is completed (19:30).[72] There is no glory apart from the cross.

Moreover, insofar as Jesus alone seeks God's glory, he stands opposed to the falsehood (7:18; 8:54–55), darkness (1:5, 9, 14) and self-seeking (5:41–44) which characterize the world below (8:23, 50). Here "glory" designates Jesus' character in radical antithesis to the character of the world. Just as the world's true nature is manifested in its rejection of God and the one whom he has sent, so Jesus' nature is manifested in his unity with God. In this sense Jesus is truly always "on the side of God," one with him, and so manifests God's glory. But although such statements imply that Jesus is not "of this world" (i.e. manifesting its character), they certainly cannot be taken to mean that Jesus does not fully enter into this world (1:5, 9, 14; 3:16). Inasmuch as the realm below is characterized by lies, darkness, and rebellion, such features could not depict a "humiliated" Christ who comes from above. John does not juxtapose glory and humiliation; he rather contrasts light, truth, love, and obedience—all encapsulated in the word "glory"—to darkness, falsehood, hate, and disobedience.

Although one may reject "glory in humiliation" as the epitome of the Johannine view of Jesus' death, nevertheless, one may represent the theme of the Johannine passion as "glorification in death," for Jesus' hour of glorification begins with his hour of death. The difference between the formulations "glory in humiliation" and "glorification in death" may seem minor but is important. Käsemann refuses to see Jesus' glorification as a process, but tends to speak only of the pre-existent "glory" which shines through him. But Jesus' "glory" is granted to him by God and is especially the result of God's glorification of him, even in the hour of his death. One may hesitate to call this "paradox," but one cannot as a result reject the importance of Jesus' death, for the "glory" which Käsemann so strongly emphasizes includes the "hour of death."

A second formulation which is both truer to the Fourth Gospel and to the British school of interpretation of it—which school Käsemann sharply criticizes—is that Jesus' passion shows that the life of the world is hidden in death.[73] The Fourth Gospel speaks of the love (3:16; 17:24) and life (3:14–16; 6:33, 38–39, 51; 19:34–35) which are available to the world only through Jesus' death. And it is this assertion that only Jesus' death offers life to the world that is peculiarly offensive to unbelievers (6:62). Peter is also offended, because he cannot accept Jesus' death as the necessary prerequisite for receiving the promised eternal heritage (13:8–10). Although Peter eventually does understand, as chapter 21 shows, the Jews ask, "How can this be?" (6:41, 62), for they fail to understand, are offended (6:61), do not believe (6:64), and hear not an offer of life, but only a "hard saying" (6:60). John 19:34 views the problem from a different angle: that of reminding the believing reader that since Jesus had indeed died, the Spirit and promised blessing were surely present. Life for the world results exclusively from the death of Jesus (12:24), but this declaration offends precisely because that life is hidden in the death of this man from Nazareth (6:41). Only the Father's gift of faith enables one to grasp this truth (6:65).

Thus the recognition that humiliation, weakness, and suffering are not central in John's depiction of Jesus' passion does not negate Jesus' real humanity or imply that the evangelist's Christology is "naively docetic." It is an understatement to say that the fourth evangelist assigns to Jesus' death a more significant place than Käsemann allows. Those who criticize the Fourth Gospel's passion narrative for its lack of emphasis on Jesus' humiliation and suffering tend to read it through Pauline spectacles, wishing to see John accentuate "the weakness of the cross" as does Paul.[74]

Although the Fourth Gospel does not argue as explicitly as Paul that, viewed from God's perspective, the cross is not what it seems to be, there is still a polemical purpose lying behind its presentation of Jesus' death. There is no doubt that the cross constitutes a problem. The objections of the Jews to eating Jesus' flesh (6:52, 60) and to the Messiah's "departure" (12:33–34) show that the necessity of the cross and its place in God's purpose had to be established. By insisting upon the necessity of the cross (13:8), the evangelist also underscores the unique claim that Jesus alone is life; but he is life for the world because, and only because, he dies. From his death flow cleansing and the promised Spirit (19:34–35). Resistance to the cross and Jesus' death—such as Peter's attempts to "save" Jesus (cp. 18:36)—is thus resistance to God's way of salvation, for Jesus has come "to give life to the world" (6:33, 38–39, 51). By presenting the cross as Jesus' glorification, the evangelist counters Jewish arguments that the cross negated Jesus' status as "the Christ, the Son of God" (12:34; 20:31). Thus Jesus declares that the Son of man must (*dei*) be lifted up and die on the cross, even though the Jews insist that the "Messiah remains forever" (12:32–34).[75]

Jesus' death on the cross is further understood as his sovereign and independent action and victory. Not only is this theme underscored by the passages about the good shepherd and the footwashing, but it also appears in the actual narrative of Jesus' arrest and crucifixion.[76] In short, the Johannine passion narrative "celebrates the victor who followed the unswerving cause of God to his last breath."[77] Such a portrayal would serve to assure Christian believers that Jesus' death was not merely a capricious result of human sinfulness, but constituted God's purpose to which Jesus obediently submitted. Therefore, in Jesus' death one ultimately sees the hand of God active. Reminded thus of their own share in eternal life, believers would be strengthened to follow Jesus, even to the point of death (see 12:25–26; 13:16; 15:13; 16:2–4); (so Müller, Becker, Wengst).

Thus the passion narrative addresses the situation of a community which has likely encountered antagonism towards its faith, in part because of the inexplicable event of the crucifixion. Yet John presents that crucifixion not as a scandal but as an event suffused with triumph. He does so because he views it retrospectively, from the viewpoint of Jesus' final glorification. The Gospel itself insists upon the necessity of the later interpretative viewpoint, available only after Jesus' resurrection (2:19–22; 7:37–39; 12:12–16) and the subsequent gift of the Spirit (14:15–17, 25–26; 15:26–27; 16:7–15). Thus the Gospel explicitly states that true understanding of Jesus' death, resurrection, and exaltation occur only after these events and in light of the teaching of the Spirit. In other words, as Bornkamm asserts, not only Jesus' death, but the entire Gospel as well, must be understood retrospectively (*von ruckwärts aus*), from the later vantage point of the insight given through the Spirit. John does not simply collapse the time of the earthly and exalted Jesus together, but interprets the former in light of the latter via the agency of the Paraclete.[78] Of the Gospel's retrospective viewpoint, Alan Culpepper writes:[79]

> The Johannine narrator tells the story of Jesus' ministry from the temporal perspective of a group, "we," which advocates belief in Jesus after his resurrection. The narrator therefore speaks from some point in the future within the narrative world and interprets Jesus as no contemporary observer would have been able to do. The references to what the disciples did not know at the time but discovered after Jesus' resurrection (2:22; 12:16; 13:7; and 20:9) suggest that the perspective of the believing community—should we say the Johannine community—is presented as absolutely necessary if one is to have an adequate understanding of Jesus.

In short, the later perspective is the Spirit-inspired one and, therefore, the perspective of faith (6:63). Only by means of this vantage point does one comprehend that Jesus' death brings life to the world. Thus the unbelief of the Jews, for whom Jesus' life-giving death remains a "hard saying," contrasts the faith of the disciples, who know that Jesus has "the words of life" (6:60, 68). Just as it is the confession of the community of faith that "The Word became flesh and we beheld his glory," and that the signs show Jesus to be "the Christ, the Son of God," (20:31), so too the believing community alone sees hidden in Jesus' death the life of the world. In the words of Hoskyns and Davey, "To those whose eyes have been opened, everything Jesus said or did appears translucent, bearing witness to his glory. No one saw this glory until he was risen from the dead, and once he was risen, each episode, saying, discourse, or act is now seen to be significant and creates belief and manifests his glory to the believer."[80]

THE HUMANITY OF JESUS IN THE PERSPECTIVE OF THE FOURTH GOSPEL

THE HUMANITY OF JESUS

We are now in a position to summarize and reflect on the contours of the Fourth Gospel's view of Jesus' humanity. The chief finding of our exegetical analyses can be stated as follows: none of the passages examined in this study necessarily demands an interpretation which impugns the true humanity of Jesus. That the relevant passages can be so interpreted is clear from the history of exegesis. But it is my contention that such exposition misreads the Gospel as a whole. When verses or statements are taken out of context or only selected pericopes and ideas are emphasized and other equally Johannine elements are ignored, the resultant picture misrepresents the Gospel and its portrayal of Jesus.

One misrepresentation of the Gospel's Christology is the claim that it presents Jesus as "God going about on earth," so gloriously divine that it scarcely makes sense to speak of the humanity of Jesus in John. But exegesis lays such a claim to rest. Various opponents of Jesus object that he is a man who makes himself equal to God (5:18; 10:33). Such an objection makes sense only if *anthrōpos* and *theos* can be construed in contradistinction to one another—only if they represent different realities or realms. Unbelievers allege that these realities are antithetical and mutually exclusive: Jesus' humanity implies that he is only human. The Gospel repudiates that allegation, but not by denying Jesus' humanity or by removing him from the human sphere: Jesus' solidarity with humanity is not impugned. His heavenly glory does not simply overshadow the earthly reality nor does it shine through the humanity of the earthly Jesus as a light through a transparent veil.

The Hiddenness of Revelation

The reality that Jesus has come from God, from above, is hidden within the one whom unbelief rejects but faith confesses. In Bultmann's terms, God's revelation is present "in a peculiar hiddenness" precisely because of Jesus' undeniable humanity.[1] Nevertheless, with Käsemann one must reject Bultmann's formulation "the revealer is nothing but a man" as a summary of the Gospel's theme. On the one hand, while Bultmann stresses the "sheer humanity" of the Revealer, the Gospel presupposes that humanity and emphasizes that it is this man who makes God known. On the other hand, the phrase "nothing but a man" does not adequately characterize John's view of Jesus.

In affirming Jesus' humanity, the Gospel does not hesitate to speak of Jesus as *sarx* (flesh). "Flesh" is a hindrance to faith because it connotes that which is earthly and human and, consequently, in contrast to God, who is heavenly and divine. Flesh is perishable, but God is eternal; flesh is human, but God is holy (Isa. 40:6–8; Ps. 145:21). And yet the Gospel speaks of Jesus' flesh in contexts which juxtapose it specifically to his heavenly origins, without apparent conflict, incongruity, or tension. Thus John 1:14 points to the fact that the Word came from God (1:1–2), became *sarx*, and dwelt as a human being "among us." John 6:51–58 emphasizes that the sacrifice of the flesh of Jesus in his death is in truth God's gift of heavenly bread, the bread of life. And when the Gospel testifies to Jesus' authority over "all flesh" (17:2), one sees again the inherent contrast between heaven (17:1) and earth (17:4). The evangelist does not soften the offense of Jesus' flesh: through it God is seen (1:14, 18) and salvation is offered (6:52).

Thus "flesh" denotes Jesus' human existence in this world in terms which elsewhere in John connote that which is natural, earthly, and human. In other words, when the Gospel asserts "the Word became flesh" it explicitly defines Jesus in terms that are used of other human beings (17:2). Because "flesh" can in certain contexts designate that which stands in antithesis to God, statements about the flesh of Jesus also place him unmistakably within the earthly and human realm. It is in this sense that one must interpret *kai ho logos sarx egeneto*: although Jesus is himself God's Word, he enters into that realm which stands over against God and becomes *sarx*, human, flesh. The subsequent phrase, "we beheld his glory" accordingly means that Jesus' human life and death are the place of revelation. That Jesus reveals God is not contradicted by Jesus' humanity; that Jesus reveals God does not efface Jesus' humanity.

Jesus' Humanity and *Sēmeia*

Yet it is certainly not true that for the fourth evangelist Jesus is "nothing but a man." Typically Jesus' miracle-working is understood as an extraordinary activity which distinguishes and separates him from the rest of humanity. That Jesus "did signs" constitutes part of his uniqueness for the fourth evangelist (15:24), but that uniqueness may not be construed in such a way that it negates Jesus' humanity.

In designating Jesus' miracles as *sēmeia* the evangelist intends them to be understood as something more than acts of power (*dynameis*). As "signs" they point to and reveal Jesus' identity. Yet the signs are not arbitrary pointers, functioning independently of the actual deed which Jesus does. The bare fact that Jesus does signs is significant, but that he does *certain* signs is equally important. When Jesus opens the eyes of a blind man, that deed reveals Jesus as the light of the world; when Jesus raises Lazarus, he is manifested as the resurrection and the life. Not only do the signs point beyond themselves to the reality of who Jesus is, but they do so by effecting material changes in this world. As acts affecting the material world, they are not only "spiritual" or "symbolic"; they are not merely "pointers" (*Hinweise*). Rather, through them Jesus offers gifts to human beings. "Just as there is glory to be seen in the flesh, so the mundane can point to a higher reality, which Jesus both embodies and reveals to those who will believe in him."[2]

Inasmuch as signs are deeds affecting the material world, they reveal one who is part of and works in this world. It is precisely these deeds which call for faith in Jesus. Jesus is known on the basis of "solidly material" deeds; he is known in and through earthly realities. One is constantly referred to the miracle itself and, accordingly, to the one who actually performed it. The signs are not removed from their setting within the ministry of Jesus, as the reminder that Jesus did these signs "in the presence of his disciples" makes clear. Although Jesus' signs depict heavenly or spiritual realities, they do so through that which is material and historical. And as the one who did these signs, Jesus is known through and in them.

That the signs are "solidly material" deeds through and in which Jesus is known suggests that they ought to bring those who see them to a knowledge of him. But, as the Gospel makes clear, not all who see them believe. Thus the evangelist writes, "Even though he had done so many signs before them, yet they did not believe" (12:37). Although some "saw his glory" (1:14; 2:11), others remained blind (9:41). Again one confronts the hiddenness of revelation. Even the signs are not accessible as revelation to all. The revelation in the signs is not hidden arbitrarily, but because signs are deeds done by a human being. Throughout the Gospel Jesus repeatedly asserts that he works not by his own power and authority, but by God's, and not by his own will, but in submission to that of the Father. But for the unbeliever, Jesus' assertion that his works are the works of the Father is tantamount to a claim of equality with God (5:18; 10:33). The offense of the signs lies in the fact that the one who does them claims that they reveal his own unity with God, and thus ultimately God himself (5:19–20, 36; 10:25, 32, 37–38). On the one hand, the signs do not efface Jesus' humanity, because he does them only by virtue of his relation to and dependence on the Father. On the other hand, the signs underscore the claim that the works of this human being reveal God's own activity (10:38; 14:10–11).

Jesus' Death and the Powers
of this World

Jesus' death places him firmly in this world. By portraying that death as the result of the forces of this world, the Gospel shows that Jesus has entered fully into that human, fleshly, material world. He is subject to the powers of this world in his betrayal and crucifixion, even though that death happens of his own volition and by the will of God (14:30; 18:11, 30–32, 35–36; 19:11). While Jesus' death happened at the behest of the Father (10:18), the forces of evil (as represented by the "ruler of this world") are at work as well (6:70–71; 13:2; 14:30). So also Jesus' disciples remain "in this world" of the evil one, where they will experience enmity, persecution, tribulation, and death, even though they are "not of the world" and even though Jesus has "overcome the world" (15:18–19; 16:2, 33; 17:11, 14–15). Jesus' triumph in death, which assures his followers' triumph, does not negate the reality of existence in this world, but assures believers that despite appearances to the contrary, Jesus has indeed "overcome the world." While Jesus' death seems to give the lie to his claims—just as Jesus' human origins and flesh seem to indicate that he is only human—Jesus' cross was in reality the beginning of his glorification and exaltation. But that is not immediately apparent nor finally visible to all: the cross remains an offense to many (12:32–34).

Docetism and Anti-docetism in the Gospel

Jesus clearly is human: his human origins, flesh, and death are common to "all flesh"; his signs are worked in dependence on God as is appropriate to one who is flesh. The Gospel unhesitatingly places Jesus within the material, human sphere, where his signs and death effect life and salvation. Consequently it is a misreading of the Gospel to label it "naively docetic." If the Gospel is interpreted in its entirety and on its own terms, such a judgment cannot be supported exegetically, for the Gospel neither obliterates the humanity of Jesus nor repudiates his solidarity with the world and its inhabitants.[3]

It is, therefore, not appropriate to call the Christology of the Fourth Gospel either "docetic" or "naively docetic" if those terms are understood as characterizing a Jesus who is not truly part of this world. In fact, many exegetes (e.g. Thyen, Langbrandtner, Richter, Bernard, Hoskyns, Lindars, Morris) have argued in just the opposite direction. They have argued that the Gospel—or parts

of it, notably John 1:14—insists on the reality of Jesus' humanity
and flesh, and is actually anti-docetic, combatting either the kind of
view of Jesus which Käsemann delineates in *The Testament of Jesus*
or an even more emphatic denial of his true incarnation. But "anti-
docetic" does not sum up adequately the Gospel's thrust.[4] It does
not set out to prove that Jesus was truly human or that he possessed
a real body of flesh and blood. Instead, this is exactly what the
Gospel assumes. On this assumption it builds its argument that the
one who became flesh was indeed God's Word; that the one who
did signs revealed the glory of God; and that the ignominious death
on the cross was in reality the will of God and the beginning of
Jesus' exaltation. The accent falls on "seeing" those earthly realities
with eyes of faith, so that one truly "sees" (perceives) who Jesus
is. To be sure, emphasis on Jesus' flesh constitutes an essential part
of John's polemic, but that polemic is directed not against those
who deny the reality of the incarnation but against those who deny
that one sees the activity and revelation of the one true God in
Jesus' life and death.

Those who find an anti-docetic polemic in the Gospel often read
it through the spectacles of the Epistle of First John. As a result,
the polemic in that Epistle—which clearly insists on the importance
of the statement that Jesus has come in the flesh (4:2)—is too easily
read back into the situation of the Gospel. But the Gospel's emphasis falls elsewhere. The Gospel declares that in the flesh of Jesus,
God is revealed; the Epistle, that God is revealed in the *flesh* of
Jesus.

THE QUESTION OF PERSPECTIVE

If neither "docetic" nor "anti-docetic" sums up the thrust of the
Gospel's polemic, what can be said about the purpose behind the
Johannine presentation of Jesus? Against Käsemann's description
of John's Christology as "naively docetic," Nicol argued that John
is thoroughly conscious that his "high Christology" represents a
later interpretation under the Spirit's guidance.[5] Nicol's formulation of the problem raises the question of John's theological perspective: Does the evangelist himself regard his account as a portrait

of the earthly Jesus? Granted that John portrays Jesus as sovereign and triumphant, can one account for these features in light of John's retrospective viewpoint? Or can these features be explained in terms of John's purpose? Numerous recent studies have argued persuasively that the development of Johannine Christology must be linked to the historical situation which produced the Gospel (Thyen, Richter, Wengst, Brown, Martyn). If this situation can be deduced from the Gospel, we may well be aided in understanding why John formulates his Christology as he does. To conclude this study of the humanity of Jesus in John, I offer some suggestions about the Gospel's perspective and purpose, recognizing that even when these have been fully explored—which cannot be done here—the problem of the uniqueness of John's presentation of Jesus remains: "The historical circumstances which produced the Johannine presentation of Jesus are important for understanding it, but they do not really 'explain' it, nor can they be substituted for it."[6]

The Retrospective Viewpoint

Of primary significance in interpreting the Fourth Gospel's presentation of Jesus is the recognition that it does not simply obliterate the distinction between the time of Jesus and the time of the Church. Throughout the Gospel there are allusions to a fuller understanding of events available only after Jesus' death, resurrection, and the subsequent gift of the Spirit. Explicitly included among those things which will be understood later are Jesus' death and resurrection (2:19–22; 12:16; 13:7; 20:9), the Scriptures (2:17, 22; 12:16), interpretations of Jesus' own words (2:22; 7:37–39), and the giving of the Spirit (7:37–39). Crucial events of Jesus' life (his words, his death and resurrection) and their relationship to the Scriptures are grasped in their full meaning only after the events.

The Gospel appeals explicitly to Scripture when it declares that certain events of Jesus' life and ministry happened as the fulfillment of Scripture (2:17; 12:37–40; 13:18; 19:24, 30, 36). That the various Old Testament *testimonia* justify circumstances which could prove problematic for the Church's affirmation of Jesus as Messiah and Lord (such as his rejection by the Jews, his betrayal by Judas, and his crucifixion) shows the probable apologetic function of such texts as these. Their origin within the community of faith is also demonstrated by the fact that the fuller understanding of Scripture or the events of Jesus' ministry is specifically to be possessed by Jesus' disciples (2:17, 19–22; 12:16; 13:7; 20:9) or those who believed in him (7:37–39). A correct perception of Jesus' life and death is not available to all, but only to those who follow him as disciples. Because discipleship is defined as abiding (*menein*), it is clear that those who remain faithful are those who understand. Proper perception of Jesus' life belongs only to the believing community.

But by demonstrating that the circumstances of Jesus' life fulfilled the Scriptures, the author also shows that only the believing community properly interprets Scripture.[7] A correct interpretation of the significance of Jesus' life, death, and resurrection is bound together with a correct interpretation of the Scriptures: both are available only within the community of faith. Therefore it is only the disciples who are not offended by Jesus' origins (1:45; 6:42; 7:31, 41–52), by his flesh (1:14; 6:51–69), and by his death (6:51–59). Likewise, it is only the disciples who see his glory (1:14; 2:11).

Various passages in chapter 17, although they are spoken by Jesus before his departure to the Father, look back on his earthly work as an event in the past and thus manifest the same retrospective viewpoint. Jesus views his work as accomplished (17:4), even though it is quite clear that the cross, which is yet ahead, actually fulfills his mission (19:30). Similarly, he views his mission as over, asserting, "I glorified thee on earth," and "I am no more in the world" (17:11)—although he himself is not yet with the Father (20:17). Again, his declaration "I have manifested thy name" (17:6, 26) must be balanced by the petition for God to glorify his name through Jesus' death and exaltation (12:28). By showing that Jesus himself looked back on and explained the meaning of his work on earth before his departure (death), the Gospel finds the foundation for its interpretation in Jesus himself. The passages throughout the Gospel where Jesus explains his betrayal and death similarly show that the community's understanding is no creation *de novo*, but is rooted in the words and deeds of Jesus himself.

In sum, the Gospel's viewpoint can be called *retrospective* in that it views the events of Jesus' life from a later vantage point, and *ideological* in the sense that it narrates those events from a definite theological stance; both are necessary for understanding.[8] Although the evangelist's viewpoint depends on the passage of time, it depends still more immediately (as he himself makes clear) on the Paraclete's teaching and inspiration. The Spirit's coming is subsequent to Jesus' glorification and return to the Father (7:39; 20:22). This Spirit belongs specifically to the community of faith (14:17); he teaches them "all things" (14:26; 16:13), brings to their memory the words Jesus spoke while on earth (14:26; 15:26), and speaks of what is yet to come (16:13). The knowledge which belongs to the community of faith is the result of the Spirit's revelation. The Spirit's revelatory witness belongs to those whom the Father has drawn (6:44), given to Jesus (6:37), and taught (6:45).

The Post-Easter Perspective

Because the Gospel acknowledges the function of the Spirit in guiding the disciples "into all truth" as well as the fact that the Spirit was given only after Jesus' death (7:39), there is a reserve about the application of certain predicates to Jesus within the earthly ministry. While the prologue (1:1–18) speaks of Jesus as "God" and "Logos," it is not until Jesus breathes the Spirit upon the disciples that we again have a parallel confession in Thomas' words, "My Lord and my God!" Such confessions of faith are fitting in introducing the Gospel and appropriate after Easter, but clearly the man from Nazareth cannot simply be called a glorious "god on earth" apart from that post-resurrection faith perspective.

It is within this context that one must understand John's portrait of Jesus. In view of the fact that the evangelist specifically points to his later, post-resurrection vantage point, derived from the Spirit's teaching and accessible only to faith, it is quite clear that he does not understand his account as a biographical portrait of the earthly Jesus. That is not to imply that he has created *ex nihilo* all the material of the Gospel or that he views the earthly Jesus or history as irrelevant; our analyses of the Gospel's treatment of Jesus' origins, signs, flesh, and death suggest otherwise. Rather it is to say that through the agency of the Spirit he has interpreted the significance of Jesus for his community, and that the post-Easter confession of Jesus as Lord (20:28) colors his narrative. Yet the evangelist does not use the earthly ministry "merely as a backdrop" for the story of God's appearance on earth; he does not evacuate it of its historical reality but interprets Jesus' presence and significance for his community through his later perspective.

These insights into John's perspective suggest that we must be careful in framing our descriptions of John's portrait of Jesus. John consciously interprets from a post-Easter perspective, from which Jesus is now understood as glorified and exalted. In this light, Christology can be nothing other than a "Christology of glory" or "exaltation." But if either phrase is taken to imply that John indiscriminately reads this Christology back into the life of the earthly Jesus, then that phrase is inadequate because it misrepresents the Gospel. The evangelist acknowledges not only the distinction between the glory Jesus manifested on earth and that which he has upon his return to the Father, and thereby the distinction between the earthly Jesus and exalted Lord, but also that only the Spirit's presence enabled full perception of Jesus' identity. Thus the glory which Jesus manifests in no way obliterates his real humanity.

The Conflict of Belief and Unbelief

Such a view of Jesus' life and death arises not out of a docetizing tendency, but out of a situation where the realities of Jesus' existence in this world are used as weapons against Christian claims. The situation is most likely that of a conflict between the evangelist's community and its Jewish antagonists. The Gospel's chief polemic is aimed against those who reject God's Son, thereby also rejecting their opportunity of becoming true children of Abraham and, ultimately, true children of God (1:12–13; 8:39–42). Unbelievers do not see that Jesus is God's Son and Messiah (20:31), the one promised in Scripture (1:46; 5:46) who is greater than Moses (1:18; 6:32), Jacob (4:12), and Abraham (8:53–59), and who supersedes both the revelation given through the Jewish law (1:18; 5:46) and the Jewish religious feasts and rituals (2:1–11, 19–22; 7:37–39). Such arguments imply a situation in which the interpretation of Jesus' relationship to the Scriptures and Judaism was disputed and in which the Johannine community sought justification for its claim by appealing to the Scriptures and the testimony of the Spirit. As Whitacre writes, "By showing Jesus to be the fulfillment of Scripture, the author assures his readers in their faith in Jesus; in following Jesus they are loyal to the God revealed in Judaism."[9]

In his treatment of Jesus' origins, the evangelist also reassures his readers by showing that it is not the facts of Jesus' earthly heritage that are the obstacle but rather the lack of perception and belief. Faith sees in the man from Nazareth the one whom God has sent, the Messiah and Son of God. While the prologue polemicizes against those who do not recognize Jesus as God's unique Son, it also assures believers that "in him is life." Eternal life is secured only by Jesus' death, which offends unbelievers but not those who abide as disciples. Similarly, the signs are proofs of Jesus' identity and thus evoke belief; but while many believed "because of the signs," only those disciples who remained faithful truly saw Jesus' glory. The sharp lines drawn between believers and unbelievers, and between faithfulness to Jesus (= knowledge of God) and rejection of him (= rejection of God) suggest a radically polarized and irreconcilable division focused, quite obviously, on the identity of Jesus. Thus the Gospel aims both to remind believers that in Jesus alone is God made known (1:18) and to account for unbelief, and thereby to explain the division and conflict that are part of the believers' everyday experience.

"My Lord and My God!"

In the service of its polemic, the Gospel affirms Jesus' divine identity in the strongest possible terms: not only does one see the revelation of God in Jesus, Jesus is confessed as "God" (1:1; 20:29). That confession brings us back to the problem of Jesus' humanity. Once Jesus is confessed as God, can there be any real sense in which he can be said to be human? Does not that confession obliterate his humanity? On the evangelist's terms the answer to the first question is yes, and to the second question, no. In confessing Jesus as "God" the Fourth Gospel never denies Jesus' humanity. In fact, in arguing that in Jesus' life and death one sees God active, the Gospel is unyielding in its demands that one look at the one who was flesh, who performed signs among them, and who died on a

Roman cross. In this Gospel one reads alongside Jesus' statement "The Father and I are one" (10:30) his assertion that "the Father is greater than I" (14:28). Either of these statements could be taken as the leitmotif of John's Christology and used to interpret the other, as the history of exegesis amply demonstrates. Yet John holds them together.

How Jesus can be both God and man, in some sense equal with God and yet in another sense distinctly subordinate to him, was the problem that the Church wrestled with especially in the fourth and fifth centuries. How John holds these together is the question that still troubles exegetes of the Fourth Gospel. That he was unable to do so, but gave precedence to the dogmatic formulation, "I and the Father are one," is the contention of Käsemann and his forebears in interpreting the Gospel. In Wrede's terms, the Jesus of the Fourth Gospel is a "wandering God"; in Käsemann's, "God striding across the earth." The corollary of that view is that a Gospel which depicts Jesus in that way can not be called anything other than "naively docetic."

This brings us full circle to the dilemma of defining "humanity." We have endeavored to allow the Gospel to define Jesus' humanity on its own terms, and the result can be summed up as follows: although Jesus shares his humanity in common with all other human beings, that humanity does not finally limit or define him; nevertheless, his uniqueness or *un*likeness does not efface his humanity. It is that *un*likeness which is disconcerting. And yet, as S. W. Sykes asks:[10]

> Can one assert *both* that there is nothing remarkable about his history *and* yet that it points through to the absolute so that man could conclude that to have seen Jesus was to have seen the Father? Any account which does not distinguish [Jesus] from the rest of humanity is not credible as christology; and any account which does so distinguish him is clearly not merely "normal" or "empirical" humanity.

In other words, for Jesus to be truly human must he be exactly and only like all other humans? The answer of the fourth evangelist to that question is no. He does accept Jesus' humanity; but he also confesses that he who was known as the "son of Joseph" is the Son of God, that he who became flesh is the Word of God, that he who performed signs is the light of the world and bread from heaven, and that he who died on the cross is the resurrection and the life.

ABBREVIATIONS

AnBib	Analecta Biblica
ANRW	*Aufstieg und Niedergang der römischen Welt*
ATR	*Anglican Theological Review*
BEvT	Beiträge zur evangelischen Theologie
BSR	Biblioteca di scienze religiose
BU	Biblische Untersuchungen
BZ	*Biblische Zeitschrift*
CBQ	*Catholic Biblical Quarterly*
CurTM	*Currents in Theology and Mission*
ExpTim	*Expository Times*
ICC	International Critical Commentary
Int	*Interpretation*
JBL	*Journal of Biblical Literature*
JTC	*Journal for Theology and the Church*
KD	*Kerygma und Dogma*
LCC	Library of Christian Classics
NovT	*Novum Testamentum*
NovTSup	Novum Testamentum, Supplements
NTAbh	Neutestamentliche Abhandlungen
NTS	*New Testament Studies*
QD	Quaestiones Disputatae
SANT	Studien zum Alten und Neuen Testament
SBLDS	Society of Biblical Literature Dissertation Series

SE   *Studia Evangelica*
SNTSMS   Society for New Testament Studies Monograph Series
ThR   *Theologische Rundschau*
USQR   *Union Seminary Quarterly Review*
ZNW   *Zeitschrift für die neutestamentliche Wissenschaft*

NOTES

INTRODUCTION:
THE PROBLEM OF JESUS'
HUMANITY IN THE FOURTH GOSPEL

1. References are to Käsemann's *Jesu letzter Wille nach Johannes 17*, rev. ed. (Tübingen: J. C. B. Mohr [Paul Siebeck], 1971); direct quotations are from the English trans. of the first (1966) German ed. (Philadelphia: Fortress Press, 1968).

2. See e.g. Bultmann, *The Gospel of John*, 62 n. 4, 64, 68; idem, *Theology of the New Testament* 2:40.

3. See esp. Käsemann, *Letzter Wille*, 21–23, 27–28, 42–43, 51.

4. Ibid., 61–62.

5. See Bornkamm's review article "Towards the Interpretation of John's Gospel: A Discussion of *The Testament of Jesus* by Ernst Käsemann (1968)," 86–95; and Koester, *Introduction to the New Testament*. Koester's argument reads like a defense of Bultmann against Käsemann (2:190).

6. Among others, see the comments by Thyen in "Aus der Literatur zum Johannesevangelium," *ThR* 39 (1974): 236–37; see also Kysar, *The Fourth Evangelist and His Gospel*, 191; and Wengst, *Bedrängte Gemeinde und verherrlichter Christus*, 98–101.

7. See Smith, *The Composition and Order of the Fourth Gospel*, 57–115.

8. Smalley, *John: Evangelist and Interpreter*, 55. Koester (comment in "Seminar Dialogue") also protests against Käsemann's use of John 17 as the theological vantage point for interpreting the Gospel.

9. In questioning the assessment of the Gospel as "naively docetic" over against the Synoptic Gospels, Johnson (*The Writings of the NT*, 475) notes, "The contrast, however, can be overdrawn. Jesus is scarcely just another

131

human being in Mark's Gospel. John's is in many ways the most human portrayal of Jesus."

10. Smalley, *John: Evangelist and Interpreter*, 55–56 (my emphasis).

11. A summary of the viewpoints of these scholars and their points of contact with Käsemann can be found in my dissertation, "The Humanity of Jesus in the Gospel of John," 17–23.

12. Käsemann, *Testament*, 9.

13. Ibid., 10.

14. Ibid., 45.

15. Meeks, review of Käsemann's *Testament*, *USQR* 24 (1969): 419. For similar skepticism about the applicability of "docetic" and "anti-docetic" in referring to the Johannine writings, see Thyen, "Aus der Literatur," *ThR* 44 (1979): 110 n. 25. Käsemann remains unimpressed. See his response to Meeks, as well as to Bornkamm's charge of anachronism, in *Letzter Wille*, 61 n. 68, 62 n. 69, as well as the comments appended to the translation of Bornkamm's "Towards the Interpretation of John's Gospel."

16. This is the position of Schottroff in *Der Glaubende und die feindliche Welt*.

17. This is the argument of Thyen in numerous articles, and of his pupil Langbrandtner in *Weltferner Gott oder Gott der Liebe?*

18. Explicitly or implicitly, this is established by Schottroff in *Der Glaubende und die feindliche Welt*, and by Langbrandtner in *Weltferner Gott oder Gott der Liebe?*

19. Käsemann, *Testament*, 7.

20. De Jonge, *Jesus: Stranger from Heaven and Son of God*, vii–viii.

21. See the appreciative but critical comments of Wengst in *Bedrängte Gemeinde*, 19–20.

22. Nicholson (*Death as Departure*, 14–17) and Whitacre (*Johannine Polemic*, 3–4) have also adopted the compositional integrity of the text as a working hypothesis, although Nicholson regards John 1—20 as the basic object of investigation.

23. Culpepper, *Anatomy of the Fourth Gospel*, 5. For Culpepper, "literary criticism" denotes the study of the Gospel through the methods of the discipline of literary criticism. In that regard, it must be distinguished from "literary criticism" which analyzes the Gospel's use of sources, stylistic characteristics, and possible displacements in composition. It is this latter usage that Schnackenburg has in mind when he discusses literary criticism of the Gospel in the introduction to his commentary, *The Gospel according to St. John* 1:47–58.

24. Culpepper, *Anatomy*, 49 n. 65.

25. See Lieu, "Gnosticism and the Gospel of John," *ExpTim* 90 (1979): 233.

26. See e.g. Mussner, *The Historical Jesus in the Gospel of St. John*.

27. For an analysis of the relationship of Jesus (the Son) to God (the Father) and a discussion of Jesus' deity, see Fennema, "Jesus and God according to John."

28. On this topic, see Taylor, "Does the New Testament Call Jesus God?" 83–89; Brown, "Does the New Testament Call Jesus God?" 1–38; Mastin, "A Neglected Feature of the Christology of the Fourth Gospel," *NTS* 22 (1975): 32–51; and Fennema, "John 1:18; 'God the Only Son,' " *NTS* 31 (1985): 124–35.

CHAPTER ONE: THE ORIGINS OF JESUS

1. The referent of the term "the Jews" in the Fourth Gospel has received considerable attention. For summaries of the state of the discussion, see Culpepper, *Anatomy*, 125–32; and Wengst, *Bedrängte Gemeinde*, 37–44. While "the Jews" are representatives of unbelief in the Gospel (Culpepper, *Anatomy*, 129), it must be remembered that Jesus and his disciples were Jewish and that, according to John, "salvation is of the Jews" (4:22). Hence, "the Jews" are "types" or "symbols" of unbelief, not because of their national heritage, but because they are, as recent scholarship has persuasively argued, the actual opponents of the evangelist and his community, just as they were, quite obviously, Jesus' contemporaries. More than likely the Johannine community included a large number of Jewish Christians, who found themselves in a bitter theological and sociological conflict with their neighbors, Jews who did not accept the Christian affirmations about Jesus.

2. Bultmann, *Theology of the NT* 2:41.

3. Schottroff, *Der Glaubende und die feindliche Welt*, 268–71.

4. While Philip does not speak explicitly of the Messiah, most commentators equate his statement about "him of whom Moses in the law and also the prophets wrote" (1:45) with the promised Messiah; so Barrett, *The Gospel according to St. John*, 184; Bultmann, *The Gospel of John*, 103 n. 4; Dodd, *The Interpretation of the Fourth Gospel*, 228; Haenchen, *A Commentary on the Gospel of John* 1:165; and Schnackenburg, *John* 1:315. Brown (*The Gospel according to John* 1:86) thinks the statement refers more generally to Jesus as the fulfillment of the entire OT.

5. Thus some scholars find 1:45–46 parallel to 7:41 and 7:52, where the objection to Galilee is explicitly stated; so e.g. Barrett, *John*, 184; Haenchen, *John* 1:166–67; and Lindars, *The Gospel of John*, 118.

6. Bultmann, *John*, 103 n. 7, 104.

7. Schnackenburg, *John* 1:315. Schnackenburg writes that Nathanael's objection, like that of 6:42, reflects "the scandal given by the appearance of the Messiah in the flesh, when not met with faith." While it is difficult to pin down precisely what the objection to Nazareth is, the problem is occasioned neither by Galilee nor by scriptural proof that the Messiah must

be born elsewhere but simply by the low opinion in which Nazareth is held. Lindars (*John*, 117) links together the appellation "son of Joseph" with the question about Nazareth and suggests the former implies the insignificance of Jesus' family.

8. See Hooker, "The Johannine Prologue and the Messianic Secret," *NTS* 21 (1974): 40–58; and Culpepper, *Anatomy*, 19, 32–36, 57, 89, 151.

9. Brown, *John* 1:186–88; Bultmann, *John*, 204; Haenchen, *John* 1:234; and Schnackenburg, *John* 1:462–64.

10. Bultmann, *John*, 204.

11. Brown, "The Problem of Historicity in John," 158.

12. Meeks argues that the pronoun *idios* in the phrase "his own country" (*en tē idia patridi*), which contrasts with the synoptic use of the personal pronoun *heautou*, is a deliberate Johannine construction parallel to 1:11. Jesus' *patris*—Judea—is his "own country," but *not* his "native country," which is Galilee. In the Fourth Gospel, Jerusalem is the place of judgment and rejection, while Galilee is the place of acceptance and discipleship. See Meeks' discussions in *The Prophet-King*, 39–41, and in "Galilee and Judea in the Fourth Gospel," *JBL* 85 (1966): 159–69. See, however, the objections raised by Dodd in his cautious assessment of this passage in *Historical Tradition in the Fourth Gospel*, 239. For further discussion of the possible theological significance of topography in John, see, in addition to Meeks and Dodd, Davies, *The Gospel and the Land*, 288–335; Fortna, "Theological Use of Locale in the Fourth Gospel," *ATR* supp. ser. (1974): 58–95; and Reim, "John IV.44—Crux or Clue?" *NTS* 22 (1976): 476–80. The recent discussion by Pryor ("John 4:44 and the *Patris* of Jesus," *CBQ* 49 [1987]: 254–63) comes to a conclusion similar to mine.

13. E.g. Brown, *John* 1:313; Dodd, *Interpretation*, 89; Lindars, *John*, 293; and Haenchen, *John* 2:15–16.

14. The most important pseudepigraphal passages are 2 *Bar.* 29:3; 39:7; 73:1; 4 *Ezra* 7:28; 12:32; 13:26, 32, 52; 14:9; 1 *Enoch* 48:6–7; 62:7. The translations are from *The Old Testament Pseudepigrapha*, ed. Charlesworth. For a discussion of the Messiah in these documents, see Charlesworth, "The Concept of the Messiah in the Pseudepigrapha," in *ANRW* 19/1:188–218.

15. O'Neill, "The Silence of Jesus," *NTS* 15 (1969): 166.

16. Ibid. O'Neill argues that part of the messianic ideal was the Messiah's silence with respect to his own identity until God should choose to reveal him, and suggests that this may account for the "messianic secret" in the Gospels.

17. Justin Martyr *Dialogue with Trypho* 8.4; see also 110.1.

18. So e.g. Barrett, *John*, 322. In reference to Justin's statement, Barrett writes: "This however does not amount to much more than saying: 'The

Messiah will not be known until he is known,' and is not a full parallel to the words in John, which imply that when the Messiah is known to be Messiah it will still not be known whence he has come." Similarly cautious is de Jonge (*Jesus: Stranger from Heaven*, 90–91), who comments that it is "possible that the tradition of 'the hidden Messiah' is also hinted at in 7:27." He also notes that the main emphasis in the tradition as found in the Pseudepigrapha and in Justin is the contrast between "first hidden" and "finally revealed" and that in the two earliest forms of this tradition there is no emphasis on the *place* where the Messiah is hidden.

19. In discussing Jewish messianic expectations in general and objections to Jesus as the Messiah within the Fourth Gospel, de Jonge (*Jesus: Stranger from Heaven*, 78–79) states:

> Our primary task, therefore, is to investigate how these references to Jewish (or Samaritan) beliefs function in the setting in which they occur, and within the Gospel as a whole. . . . We cannot use the Johannine material without taking into account that the Jews, whose opinion is expressed in the Gospel, appear on a scene set by a Christian evangelist. . . . If statements made by Jewish opponents or sympathizers in the Fourth Gospel do not agree with expressions or conceptions found in Jewish sources, or show only partial agreements, we may not exclude the possibility that the Gospel, as our only source, has preserved truly Jewish notions and beliefs. After all, the Jewish material is variegated, and very scanty and haphazard. Yet the Johannine material can only be used to fill in the gaps or to correct the picture after due allowance has been made for its function within the Fourth Gospel.

20. See the discussion in Meeks' *The Prophet-King*, 32–35.

21. Barrett (*John*, 330) is "confident that John was aware of the tradition that Jesus was born at Bethlehem." Even though Jesus was brought up in Galilee, he was not born there. Brown (*John* 1:330) and Schnackenburg (*John* 2:158–59) also hold that at 7:41 there is an ironic allusion to Jesus' birth in Bethlehem. Contrast Bultmann, *John*, 305 n. 6.

22. Wengst (*Bedrängte Gemeinde*, 99–100) comments that because the evangelist lets the well-known facts of Jesus' earthly heritage stand, they are clearly accepted by him. But one could argue that because the evangelist lets the facts stand, he does not see the value or necessity of refuting them.

23. Barrett, *John*, 184.

24. Dodd, *Interpretation*, 260 n. 1; see also Wengst, *Bedrängte Gemeinde*, 67 n. 192.

25. See e.g. Schnackenburg's excursus "The Titles of Jesus in John 1," in *John* 1:507–14; Dodd, *Interpretation*, 292; and Brown, *John* 1:77.

26. Dodd, *Interpretation*, 260.

27. Ibid. See also Lindars, *John*, 263; and Nicholson, *Death as Departure*, 166.

28. See Whitacre, *Johannine Polemic*, 69–77.

29. Ibid., 72.

30. Against Schottroff, *Der Glaubende und die feindliche Welt*, 273.

31. See Whitacre, *Johannine Polemic*, 72.

32. Recently scholars have stressed the importance of investigating the *function* of various statements regarding Jesus' identity. See e.g. Wengst, *Bedrängte Gemeinde*, 29–32; Meeks, "The Man from Heaven in Johannine Sectarianism," *JBL* 91 (1972): 44–72; and de Jonge, *Jesus: Stranger from Heaven*, 99.

33. Schnackenburg (*John* 1:315) cautiously states that the assignment of the patronymic "son of Joseph" to Jesus does not necessarily indicate the mind of the evangelist; John does not make clear the extent of his knowledge of traditions about Jesus' birth. I agree that one must be careful in assuming either too much or too little about the perspective of the evangelist at this point.

34. Meeks, *The Prophet-King*, 37. On the possibility of an ironic reference to Jesus' birth in Bethlehem, see Culpepper, *Anatomy*, 170; and Duke, *Irony in the Fourth Gospel*, 66–67.

35. See Culpepper, *Anatomy*, 170; and Duke, *Irony*, 64–69.

36. E.g. Martyn, *History and Theology in the Fourth Gospel*; Brown, *The Community of the Beloved Disciple*; and Wengst, *Bedrängte Gemeinde*, among many others.

37. As Wengst (*Bedrängte Gemeinde*, 99–101) points out. Against Bultmann's assertion that the essential function of the offense of John's Christology is its role of "calling into question" those who hear the Revealer, Wengst counters that the community was "called into question" very concretely by its external situation (16:2).

38. See Culpepper, *Anatomy*, 21–26, 151–65.

39. Hooker, "The Johannine Prologue and the Messianic Secret," *NTS* 21 (1974): 43.

40. Ibid., 45.

41. Schnackenburg, "Die Messiasfrage im Johannesevangelium," 250.

CHAPTER TWO: INCARNATION AND FLESH

1. Bultmann, *John*, 62, 141.

2. Bultmann, *Theology of the NT* 2:41–42.

3. Bultmann, *John*, 61, 62 n. 4, 63.

4. Ibid., 63.

5. Bultmann, *Theology of the NT* 2:42.

6. Bultmann (*John*, 62 n. 4) thus denies that *egeneto* indicates a physiological miracle in which the Word "became" flesh, as though the Logos was transformed from one substance to another. The Logos' appearance as the Revealer in the man Jesus is a truth which can be grasped only by

faith, and not by any other attempt—such as the doctrine of the virgin birth—to account for that paradox.

7. Bultmann, *Theology of the NT* 2:73.

8. Käsemann, "The Structure and Purpose of the Prologue to John's Gospel," 159, 161.

9. Ibid., 158.

10. Ibid., 156–59.

11. Käsemann, *Letzter Wille*, 26–28.

12. Ibid., 34, 49.

13. Käsemann especially chides the views of Anglo-Saxon interpreters such as Hoskyns, Barrett, and Sidebottom who understand John's Christology as "glory hidden in lowliness" (ibid., 32). He similarly dislikes the term "dialectic" as used e.g. by T. W. Manson (ibid., 32 n. 23). Yet he also denies that German scholars such as Bultmann and Conzelmann have succeeded in sketching John's Christology in paradoxical terms and his theology as a *theologia crucis* (ibid., 33 n. 24).

14. Smalley, " 'The Testament of Jesus': Another Look," 497.

15. Although Thyen uses terms such as "docetic" and "anti-docetic," he points out the problem of using them ("Aus der Literatur," *ThR* 44 [1979]: 110 n. 25). When he speaks of the evangelist as "anti-docetic," he means that the evangelist insists upon the complete identity of the Logos with Jesus (1:14) and that Jesus was indeed the Christ (20:31).

16. Thyen, "Aus der Literatur," *ThR* 39 (1974): 225–27, 230.

17. Käsemann ("Structure and Purpose," 160–61) writes that Bultmann's position that Jesus' "pure and simple humanity is at the heart of the Johannine concern" is not tenable. Thyen ("Aus der Literatur," *ThR* 39 [1974]: 229) justly criticizes Käsemann's delineation of Bultmann's view in these terms, since for Bultmann what lies at the heart of the Gospel is the paradox that in the purely human Jesus the eternal Logos speaks and not merely the "pure humanity" of Jesus.

18. Richter, "Die Fleischwerdung im Johannesevangelium," *NovT* 13 (1971): 105.

19. Thyen ("Aus der Literatur," *ThR* 39 [1974]: 229) states that Bultmann correctly appeals to John 1:14 as emphasizing the paradox of the disclosure of the eternal Logos in the purely human Jesus.

20. Bultmann, *John*, 59.

21. Lindars, *John*, 92; and Schnackenburg, *John* 1:263.

22. Barrett, *John*, 164; and Brown, *John* 1:12.

23. Bultmann, *John*, 60–61.

24. Ibid., 61–62.

25. Brown, *John* 1:30–31; Lindars, *John*, 93; and Schnackenburg, *John* 1:266. This is stressed by Demke in "Der Sogenannte Logos-Hymnus im johanneischen Prolog," *ZNW* 58 (1967): 53.

26. I. e. among "human beings," not the elect; so Schnackenburg, *John* 1:270. The "becoming flesh" makes possible the statement "We beheld his glory." While the "we" refers in the first place to those who have seen and believed, this does not limit the "dwelt among us" to the elect only, in that the appearance of the Word in the flesh, as a human being, made possible that some should see his glory. Cp. 17:2, in which Jesus has "power over all flesh so that he might give eternal life to all whom thou hast given him."

27. In response to Käsemann's contention that in the incarnation the Logos does not really change himself, but only his place, Barrett (" 'The Father Is Greater Than I' [Jo 14:28]," 158) says that this is a substantial concession to the description of John's Christology in terms of the paradox of "majesty veiled in humility."

28. See Barrett, *John*, 164. Käsemann ("Structure and Purpose," 157–58) writes that flesh means "what is human and earthly" though it may be viewed under various aspects. Brown (*John* 1:30–32) states that the stress on flesh in 1:14a differs somewhat from the attitude taken toward flesh in 1:13. Richter and Thyen, who think that 1:13 and 1:14 are not written by the same person, find a definite anti-docetic polemic in 1:14, which suggests that flesh has a different meaning than it does in 1:13.

29. Käsemann, "Structure and Purpose," 158.

30. Haenchen ("Probleme des johanneischen 'Prologs,' " in *Gott und Mensch*, 130–31) objects to Käsemann's interpretation because "it treats the Incarnation of the Logos as something which is self-evident, instead of as that which is unheard of, for which the wisdom-myth offers no parallel. Is it really possible that the Incarnation of the Word, which is the decisive event for the Christian community, was originally described with the words 'and the light shines in the darkness'?" Haenchen's objection rests on the assumption that the community did not speak of the coming of the Word into the world except in terms of "enfleshment," and that a Christian writer could not have referred to the incarnation as something which is "self-evident."

31. Among those who argue that there is a reference to the incarnate one already in 1:5 are Demke ("Sogenannte Logos-Hymnus," *ZNW* 58 [1967]: 56–57), Hoskyns (*The Fourth Gospel*, 143), Richter ("Fleischwerdung," *NovT* 13 [1971]: 95), Ridderbos ("The Structure and Scope of the Prologue to the Gospel of John," *NovT* 8 [1966]: 190–91), Schnackenburg (*John* 1:245–47), Schottroff (*Der Glaubende und die feindliche Welt*, 230), and Thyen ("Aus der Literatur," *ThR* 39 [1974]: 61).

32. Thyen ("Aus der Literatur," *ThR* 39 [1974]: 58) and Richter ("Fleischwerdung," *NovT* 13 [1971]: 94) concur that Käsemann's article "Structure and Purpose" made its most significant contribution precisely at this point.

33. See Schottroff, *Der Glaubende und die feindliche Welt*, 230–33; and Thyen, "Aus der Literatur," *ThR* 39 (1974): 62.

34. Thyen, "Aus der Literatur," *ThR* 39 (1974): 230.

35. Demke, "Sogenannte Logos-Hymnus," *ZNW* 58 (1967): 63; Ridderbos, "Prologue," *NovT* 8 (1966): 195.

36. Käsemann, "Structure and Purpose," 158.

37. Bultmann, *John*, 140; likewise Schnackenburg (*John* 1:371): *sarx* and *pneuma* are "two realms of being." Somewhat tentatively, Barrett (*John*, 210) concludes that "flesh" and "spirit" essentially point to human beings and God.

38. Barrett, *John*, 210; and Hoskyns, *Fourth Gospel*, 146.

39. Brown, *John* 1:138.

40. Bultmann, *John*, 281. Barrett (*John*, 338) suggests that judgment *kata sarka* means judgment "on the basis of what they see, his flesh, not allowing or conceiving that he is the word become flesh"; "flesh" refers specifically to Jesus' flesh. Schnackenburg (*John* 2:486 n. 20) doubts that such a reference is intended.

41. Schnackenburg, *John* 2:193.

42. Käsemann, "Structure and Purpose," 157; cp. the paraphrases suggested by Brown (*John* 1:340: "pass judgment according to human standards"), Hoskyns (*Fourth Gospel*, 331: "merely human judgment"), Lindars (*John*, 317: "by human methods of judicial procedure").

43. Brown, *John* 2:740; Bultmann, *John*, 492 n. 2; Hoskyns, *Fourth Gospel*, 498; Käsemann, "Structure and Purpose," 157; Lindars, *John*, 518; and Schnackenburg, *John* 3:171.

44. Brown, *John* 2:740.

45. See the comments by Becker in his updating of Thyen's *Forschungsbericht* ("Aus der Literatur [1978–80]," *ThR* 47 [1982]: 323).

46. This fact did not escape Richter's notice. He argued that because 1:14 and 6:51 equate Jesus and *sarx* and are the only two passages to do so, they must testify to an overtly anti-docetic tendency, and that because this is not the tendency of the evangelist, whose purpose to prove Jesus' other-worldly origins is manifest in 20:30–31, the verses must come from a later redactor. See Richter, "Zur Formgeschichte und literarischen Einheit von Joh 6, 31–58," in *Studien zum Johannesevangelium*, 88–119. Here, as often, Richter continues to insist that 20:30–31 provides the key to discerning the evangelist's hand and to reconstructing the struggles of the Johannine community. See the critical comments of Thyen ("Aus der Literatur," *ThR* 39 [1974]: 226; 42 [1977]: 269) and Wilckens ("Der eucharistische Abschnitt der johanneischen Rede vom Lebensbrot [Joh 6:51c–58]," 234–35).

47. Not all scholars who think that vv. 51–58 are a later addition to an earlier discourse think that they also embody a viewpoint contradictory

to or inconsistent with the earlier discourse. Brown (*John* 1:285–86) argues that vv. 51–58 belong "to the general body of Johannine tradition." Thyen ("Aus der Literatur," *ThR* 43 [1978]: 328–59) insists that whoever is responsible for the Gospel in its present form ought to be called the evangelist. This leads him to conclude that all the uses of *sarx* found in John are somehow amenable to the evangelist's theology.

48. Despite all the other arguments raised against the original unity of chap. 6, the meaning of *sarx* is the crux of the matter. If it can be shown that the usage of *sarx* accords with that in the rest of the Gospel, then the chief argument against the redactional character of 6:51c–58 falls away. See Bornkamm ("Vorjohanneische Tradition oder nachjohanneische Bearbeitung in der eucharistischen Rede Johannes 6?" 53) and Becker ("Aus der Literatur [1978–80]," *ThR* 47 [1982]: 323), who argue against the discourse's unity, and Schenke ("Die formale und gedankliche Struktur von Joh 6,26–58," *BZ* 24 [1980]: 21–41), who concludes that the discourse in its present form represents the careful composition of one hand.

49. For Bultmann's views, see *John*, 218–22, 234–37; and Smith, *Composition and Order*, 134–39. As Smith points out, Bultmann refers to 6:51b–58, while more recent exegetes generally speak of the redaction as beginning with v. 51c, since v. 51 clearly has three parts, not two. In any case the element in question is that which begins *kai ho artos de hon egō dōsō*.

50. Bultmann, *John*, 218–19.

51. Among those scholars who think that 6:51c–58 is a later addition by a redactor are Bornkamm ("Die eucharistische Rede im Johannes-Evangelium," *ZNW* 47 [1956]: 161–69), Lohse ("Wort und Sakrament im Johannesevangelium," *NTS* 7 [1960]: 110–25), Käsemann (*Letzter Wille*, 74–75), Koester ("History and Cult in the Gospel of John and in Ignatius of Antioch," 111–23), Richter ("Zur Formgeschichte und literarischen Einheit von Joh 6,31–58" [n. 46 above]), and Becker ("Aus der Literatur," *ThR* 47 [1982]: 323–25). While these scholars label 6:51c–58 as secondary, Langbrandtner (*Weltferner Gott oder Gott der Liebe?* 1–11) wants to push the beginning of the redactional addition back to v. 48; Bornkamm ("Vorjohanneische Tradition") to v. 47; and Thyen ("Aus der Literatur," *ThR* 43 [1978]: 340) to v. 45.

52. Among those who interpret v. 51c in this manner are Dunn ("John 6: A Eucharistic Discourse?" *NTS* 17 [1971]: 330, 335–36), Hoskyns (*Fourth Gospel*, 297), Lindars (*John*, 267), Schnackenburg (*John* 2:55), Schneider ("Zur Frage der Komposition von Joh 6:27–58 [59] [*Die Himmelsbrotrede*]," 134, 138), Schürmann ("Jo 6:51c—Ein Schlüssel zur grossen johanneischen Brotrede," 155–56), Schweizer ("Das johanneische Zeugnis vom Herrenmahl," 392), and Smith (*Composition and Order*, 145).

53. Barrett (" 'The Flesh of the Son of Man' [John 6:53]," in *Essays on John*, 42) calls this interpretation the "fatal weakness" of Bultmann's view. Smith (*Composition and Order*, 146 n. 84) notes that Bultmann never seems to suggest that any other interpretation of the passage is possible.

54. Clearly 6:51c echoes 6:27b–c, which speaks of the "food of eternal life, which the Son of man will give to you." Bultmann saw the problem and excised the offending part of 6:27 as redactional. Similarly, Becker (*Das Evangelium nach Johannes* 1:204) argues that the language and theology in v. 27 are like that in 6:51–58 and are, therefore, editorial; this begs the question. Schnackenburg (*John* 2:58) cautions the exegete with respect to the problem of the "hermeneutical circle" in interpreting John 6. If there are no other grounds for dismissing 6:27, an important argument against the Johannine character of 6:51c falls away, as Smith (*Composition and Order*, 142–43) makes clear.

55. Lindars, *John*, 267; and Schürmann, "Schlüssel," 161.

56. On the metaphorical nature of the language in John 6, see esp. Dunn, "John 6: A Eucharistic Discourse?" *NTS* 17 (1971): 328–38.

57. On the structure of the discourse, leading to its climactic rejection of Jesus, see Barrett, " 'Flesh of the Son of Man,' " in *Essays on John*, 40–42; Smith, *Composition and Order*, 144–45; and Schneider, "Zur Frage der Komposition," 133–34.

58. Smith, *Composition and Order*, 146; and Wilckens, "Eucharistische Abschnitt," 231, 238.

59. Schnackenburg, *John* 2:55.

60. Käsemann, "Structure and Purpose," 158.

61. Barrett, *John*, 164; and Brown, *John* 1:12.

62. Hoskyns, *Fourth Gospel*, 498; and Schnackenburg, *John* 1:267.

63. Schnackenburg, *John* 1:267.

64. Thyen, "Entwicklungen innerhalb der johanneischen Theologie und Kirche im Spiegel von Joh 21 und der Lieblingsjüngertexte des Evangeliums," 277; and Käsemann, "Structure and Purpose," 164 ("The concern of the hymn is, in any event, unequivocally and exclusively soteriological").

65. See e.g. Kysar, "Christology and Controversy," *CurTM* 5 (1978): 355.

66. In addition to the article by Kysar (n. 65), see also Hoskyns, *Fourth Gospel*, 136; and Smith, "The Presentation of Jesus in the Fourth Gospel," 288. Note Ridderbos, "Prologue," *NovT* 8 (1966): 191: "The real subject of the Prologue is not the revelation of the Logos, who also at last received form in the person of Jesus Christ. Rather the reverse: the Logos . . . is discussed under the point of view of that which has taken place in Jesus Christ and has been seen and heard in Him. In a word: Jesus Christ is, in essence, the subject of the Prologue, the Logos the predicate. And not the reverse."

67. Thyen, "Aus der Literatur," *ThR* 39 (1974): 227; idem, " 'Denn wir lieben die Brüder' (1 Joh 3,14)," 533–34; idem, "Entwicklungen, innerhalb der johanneischen Theologie," 277, 286.

CHAPTER THREE: SIGNS, SEEING, AND FAITH

1. So Wrede, *Charakter und Tendenz des Johannesevangeliums*, 6, 9, 45. One finds a similar evaluation of the Johannine *sēmeia* in Baur's *Kritische Untersuchungen über die kanonischen Evangelien, ihr Verhältnis zu einander, ihren Charakter und Ursprung*, 183, and his *Vorlesungen über neutestamentliche Theologie*, 370–72, and in Wetter's *"Der Sohn Gottes"*: *Eine Untersuchung über die Charackter und die Tendenz des Johannes-Evangeliums*, 149, 153–55, and Käsemann's *Letzter Wille*, 51–54, 112–14.

2. It is not possible to offer a complete treatment of the signs in the Fourth Gospel here. In particular, the validity of the various theories that a signs-source lies behind the Gospel cannot be treated in detail. I do not concur with Kysar's judgment that we will never know the evangelist's view of the relationship between faith and signs until we know what that relationship was in the source which he used (*The Fourth Evangelist and His Gospel*, 22). While I think it not unlikely that John had access to some sort of signs-source—i.e. a source, oral or written, which contained at least some of the miracles of Jesus—I think it very unlikely that we can recover the exact boundaries of this source and discern its theology. For similar skepticism see, among others, de Jonge, "Signs and Works in the Fourth Gospel," in *Jesus: Stranger from Heaven*, 117–18; Barrett, "Symbolism," in *Essays on John*, 65–79; and Lindars, *Behind the Fourth Gospel*, 27–42. I have traced in detail the discussion of signs in recent scholarship, esp. insofar as they bear on the question of Jesus' humanity, in my dissertation, "The Humanity of Jesus in the Gospel of John," chap. 4.

3. Schottroff, *Der Glaubende und die feindliche Welt*, 251–60. Becker also argues that signs are meaningless and superfluous for the believer ("Wunder und Christologie," *NTS* 16 [1970]: 146; "Exkurs 1, Die Semeiaquelle," in *Evangelium* 1:119). Thyen ("Entwicklungen innerhalb der johanneischen Theologie," 285; "Johannes 13 und die 'kirchliche Redaktion' des vierten Evangeliums," 347 n. 13) and Langbrandtner (*Weltferner Gott oder Gott der Liebe?* 88) find this view in the *Grundschrift* (foundational document) of John.

4. For Bultmann's view of the signs in John, see his *John*, 113, 119, 206, 208; and his *Theology of the NT* 2:44–45, 56–57, 60.

5. For Käsemann's interpretation of the Johannine view of signs, see his *Letzter Wille*, 51–54, 112–14.

6. See the excellent discussion of the Johannine signs by Schnackenburg in *John* 1:515–28.

7. Ibid. 1:525. He is responding in part to Bultmann's view that it is questionable whether the evangelist himself regarded the miracles as actual historical occurrences.

8. Haenchen, "Der Vater, der mich gesandt hat," in *Gott und Mensch*, 69; idem, "Johanneische Probleme," in *Gott und Mensch*, 88, 109; idem, *John* 1:301–2.

9. Dodd designated chaps. 1—12 as the "Book of Signs" and proposed that there were seven episodes within the book, each comprising one or more acts of Jesus and one or more interpretative discourses; see esp. *Interpretation*, 289–91, 383–89. Dodd suggests that while each episode is a relatively complete unit, all are "connected by a subtle system of cross-references and correspondences" (p. 386). It is this interconnection of themes and verbal links which makes it difficult to insist too strongly on any one outline. As Brown (*John* 1:cxlii–cxliii) comments, any proposed outline must respect the Gospel's fluidity and overlapping thought. For other outlines that explicitly attempt to link the signs and discourses, see esp. Brown, *John* 1:cxl–cxlii; and Smalley, *John: Evangelist and Interpreter*, 86–92.

10. By "signs," I believe John means what we call the miracles (e.g. the healings and feeding, thus excluding the temple cleansing; cp. 4:54) that Jesus performed during his earthly ministry (thus also excluding the catch of fish; 20:30).

11. One of the peculiarities of the Cana signs (2:1–11; 4:46–54) is the lack of explicit connection with any discourse, dispute, or debate. Jesus' discourse with Nicodemus about new life may belong with the changing of water to wine. There are thematic links between the story of the healing of the official's son, with its emphasis on Jesus' hour to give life (4:50–53), and the discourse about the Son's life-giving authority in 5:19–47 (5:21, 25–26).

12. See Barrett, *John*, 256.

13. Moule, "The Meaning of 'Life' in the Gospels and Epistles of St. John: A Study in the Story of Lazarus, John 11:1–44," *Theology* 78 (1975): 119.

14. See MacRae, "Theology and Irony in the Fourth Gospel," 88; and Minear, "The Audience of the Fourth Evangelist," 255 ("The author presents his book as a substitute for the signs, recognizing that his readers will have access to faith through reading rather than through seeing").

15. On John's narrative method, see Windisch, "Der johanneische Erzählungsstil," in *Eucharisterion* 2:174–213.

16. So Becker, "Wunder und Christologie," *NTS* 16 (1970): 146.

17. Bultmann (*John*, 131) e.g. writes, "The very fact that many people

have been brought to faith by the miracles is an indication that such faith is of doubtful value," for, he continues, "faith should not have to rely on miracles." According to Bultmann, such faith is not false, but it is a provisional, first step toward true faith, which believes apart from signs. See also Schnackenburg, *John* 1:358; and Brown, *John* 1:127.

18. On the difference between the disciples (2:11) and the many (2:23–24), Culpepper (*Anatomy*, 116) writes, "The disciples have already shown a willingness to 'follow' Jesus (1:37, 38, 40), and they remember what Jesus said (2:22). Faith which does not lead to following is therefore inadequate. 'Abiding' is the test of discipleship (cf 8:31)."

19. Barrett, *John*, 202; and Lindars, *John*, 145.

20. See Whitacre, *Johannine Polemic*, 41–42; and Culpepper, *Anatomy*, 148.

21. Schnackenburg, *John* 2:13.

22. Becker, *Evangelium* 1:190.

23. The Synoptics also report that the crowds came to Jesus because of his miracles (Mark 1:32, 37). Moreover, Matthew and Luke speak of healings in connection with the feeding of the five thousand (Matt. 14:14; cp. 15:29–31; Luke 9:11).

24. Culpepper, *Anatomy*, 135: "His confession is perceptive and entirely proper so far as it goes."

25. See Culpepper, *Anatomy*, 135, 171, 179.

26. Thus Nicodemus is not an example of the "unreliable believers" whose faith is not to be trusted (so Meeks, "The Man from Heaven in Johannine Sectarianism," *JBL* 91 [1972]: 54–55) nor of a group within the Johannine community holding the Christology of the signs-source (so Becker, *Evangelium* 1:132) nor of the "crypto-Christians" who are afraid to confess their faith publicly (so Martyn, *History and Theology*, 87; de Jonge, *Jesus: Stranger from Heaven*, 29–47; and Culpepper, *Anatomy*, 135–36). The portrayal of Nicodemus is essentially positive; see Brown, *The Community of the Beloved Disciple*, 72 n. 128.

27. Bultmann, *John*, 306.

28. Behind this verse lies the problematic question of whether the view that the Messiah would work miracles represents Jewish belief in the time of Jesus. On the one hand, Klausner (*The Messianic Idea in Israel*, 506) asserts that "the Messiah is never mentioned anywhere in the Tannaitic literature as a wonder-worker *per se*," while on the other hand, Barrett (*John*, 323) argues that it is rash to assume that no Jews expected that the Messiah would do miracles. See also Brown (*John* 1:313), who suggests the following options: (1) The idea of a miracle-working Messiah was current in NT times (cp. Mark 13:22; John 6:15). (2) Jesus' miracles forced the people to ask whether his extraordinary deeds might not mean that he was the Messiah (cp. Matt. 12:22–23). (3) The portrait of the Messiah

was influenced by the expectations of the prophet-like-Moses and Elijah, who both worked miracles; see Martyn, *History and Theology*, 93–100.

29. Schnackenburg, *John* 1:148–49. The argument is Christian, and represents John's messianic dogma, namely, that Jesus' signs reveal him to be the Messiah and Son of God (20:30–31).

30. Lindars, *John*, 405; and Duke, *Irony*, 86–87.

31. Schnackenburg, *John* 2:377.

32. Among others, Brown, *John* 1:115; Barrett, *John*, 199; Bultmann, *John*, 124–25; Fortna, *The Gospel of Signs*, 146; and Lindars, *John*, 141.

33. See also Theissen, *The Miracle Stories of the Early Christian Tradition*, 296: "Rejection of the demand for signs is not a rejection of signs. On the contrary, refusal of a sign is a punishment for unbelief, which would be nonsense if were accepted that signs were valueless. What is criticised is unbelief, not miracles. In fact, miracles are given added importance, since the reverse of the refusal of a sign is the giving of signs to faith."

34. For Becker (*Evangelium* 1:110–12) and Haenchen ("Johanneische Probleme," in *Gott und Mensch,* 88) the entire verse belongs to the source. Fortna (*Gospel of Signs*, 36–37) assigns 2:11b ("and manifested his glory") to the evangelist, the rest of the verse to the source. Schnackenburg (*John* 1:334–35) and Bultmann (*John*, 115 n. 1, 119 n. 5) attribute only the enumeration of the sign to the source.

35. Theissen's comments about the handling of the miracle traditions by NT scholars are appropriate (*Miracle Stories*, 294–95; although primarily discussing Mark, he has John, as well as the entire NT, in view): "Some doubts ... must surely be allowed, doubts whether the biblical authors dealt so unfeelingly with their traditions as many modern theologians with the biblical traditions, whether they transmitted them only to dissociate themselves from them immediately, to make them fundamentally superfluous. Can Mark really have told sixteen miracle stories solely in order to warn against belief in miracles? It seems a rather clumsy way of doing it. The alleged reservations of New Testament redactors about the miracles turn out on closer examination to be almost always reservations by modern exegetes about New Testament authors."

36. Numerous commentators have pointed out how this pericope functions as a climax to the calling of the disciples. See Brown, *John* 1:105; Schnackenburg, *John* 1:334; Becker, *Evangelium* 1:111–12; and de Jonge, *Jesus: Stranger from Heaven*, 117–40.

37. Schnackenburg (*John* 1:334–35) writes that 2:11 constitutes a "programmatic statement" of what signs are in the Fourth Gospel and of the relationship between the signs and faith.

38. So Becker, *Evangelium* 1:186–88. The evangelist repudiates miracles as a basis for faith by adapting an existing story so that it becomes an example of belief in Jesus' word. Fortna (*Gospel of Signs*, 41) states

that 4:48 "amounts *almost* to a denial of the miracle as a basis for faith" (my emphasis).

39. Bultmann (*John*, 207) says that the miracle is granted as a concession to human weakness. Cp. Barrett, *John*, 247; Haenchen, *John* 1:234–37; and Lindars, *John*, 203.

40. Schnackenburg, *John* 1:461; and Brown, *John* 1:191.

41. So Becker (*Evangelium* 1:186), who argues that 4:54a comes from the signs-source and contradicts 4:48, where the evangelist specifically rejects miracles as a basis for faith. Cp. Fortna, *Gospel of Signs*, 41.

42. Cp. Brown, *John* 1:194.

43. Schnackenburg, *John* 1:329; Brown, *John* 1:201; Lindars, *John*, 129; and Barrett, *John*, 191 ("His decisions are his own, and depend only on the Father's will").

44. On this point see Giblin, "Suggestion, Negative Response, and Positive Action in St. John's Portrayal of Jesus," *NTS* 26 (1980): 203, 205, 210–11.

45. Haenchen, *John* 1:235, 237.

46. As cited by Barrett in *John*, 249.

47. Cp. ibid., 572.

48. See Minear, "Audience of the Fourth Evangelist," 251, 255.

49. In 6:14 Jesus is hailed as a prophet, but in 6:15 the crowds wish to make him king. Meeks' suggestion (*Prophet-King*, 87–91) that the figure of Moses as a type of prophet-king underlies this change in terminology helpfully explains the present verses.

50. Ibid., 89; similarly Barrett, *John*, 278.

51. See Theissen, *Miracle Stories*, 294: "The miracles are no more criticised in John than the revealer is criticised or underplayed, not even by being misunderstood. The word of Jesus is also misunderstood (cf. Jn 3.1ff.; 7.31ff.), but that is far from making it an inadequate mode of revelation."

52. Bultmann, *John*, 217–18; Barrett, *John*, 286; Brown, *John* 1:164; Lindars, *John*, 254; and Schnackenburg, *John* 2:35.

53. Becker, *Evangelium* 1:318.

54. Bammel, " 'John Did No Miracle,' " 181–202.

55. Bultmann held that John's followers viewed him as a miracle worker, but even those who adopt Bultmann's theory of the anti-Baptist polemic of the passage deny this. See e.g. Becker, *Evangelium* 1:340.

56. Bultmann, *John*, 452; and Becker, *Evangelium* 2:408.

57. Barrett, *John*, 430.

58. Becker, *Evangelium* 2:411.

59. Becker, *Evangelium* 2:632; Brown, *John* 2:1058; Dodd, *Interpretation*, 438; Fortna, *Gospel of Signs*, 198; and Schnackenburg, *John* 2:337.

60. Becker, *Evangelium* 2:632.

61. Even though 20:25–29 does not explicitly refer to signs, it is gen-

erally cited as the epitome of this negative evaluation of "signs-faith," inasmuch as it is taken to denigrate belief which is based on sight.

62. Bultmann, *John*, 125.

63. Käsemann, *Testament*, 6, 9.

64. Käsemann, *Letzter Wille*, 27, 35.

65. Ibid., 27.

66. This tendency is much more blatant in Nicol's monograph (*The Semeia in the Fourth Gospel*). He states that Jesus' flesh does not conceal his glory but explains its visibleness and so implies a demonstration of divinity (p. 131). "The Jews do sometimes allege the humanity of Jesus as the reason that they do not believe in him (6:42, 7:27). But this is only a poor excuse by which they try to hide from the light of his divinity" (p. 133).

67. Esp. helpful are the studies by Barrett ("Christocentric or Theocentric? Observations on the Theological Method of the Fourth Gospel," in *Essays on John*) and Haenchen ("Der Vater, der mich gesandt hat," in *Gott und Mensch*).

68. Käsemann, *Letzter Wille*, 133.

69. Käsemann, *Testament*, 53: "[The Logos] acts in such a way that even in the realm of the transitory, his Word is being confirmed and signs point and call attention to his glory. Even though these signs may confuse the world, in them his own disciples experience the presence of the Good Shepherd and the door to their pasture. The Word is not without signs."

CHAPTER FOUR: THE DEATH OF JESUS

1. Käsemann, *Testament*, 7; see also his *Letzter Wille*, 29–30, 32–34, 43–51.

2. Käsemann, *Letzter Wille*, 124.

3. Richter, "Die Deutung des Kreuzestodes Jesu," in *Studien zum Johannesevangelium*, 58–73.

4. Hegermann, "Er kam in sein Eigentum: Zur Bedeutung des Erdenwirkens Jesu im vierten Evangelium," 112–31.

5. Forestell, *The Word of the Cross: Salvation as Revelation in the Fourth Gospel*.

6. Müller ("Die Bedeutung des Kreuzestodes im Johannesevangelium," KD 21 [1975]: 49–71) might be considered an exception here. Nevertheless, he holds that the evangelist does take the cross into account even though it is not the major focus of his theology and Christology (see e.g. pp. 55, 57–58, 61).

7. Becker's views are conveniently summarized in "Exkurs 8, Die Deutung des Todes Jesu im Joh," in *Evangelium* 2:401–7.

8. Bornkamm, "Towards the Interpretation of John's Gospel," 88–89.

9. Thyen develops his position in "Johannes 13," 343–56, and " 'Nie-

mand hat grössere Liebe als die, dass er sein Leben für seine Freunde hingibt' (Joh 15,13)," 467–81; cp. Wengst, *Bedrängte Gemeinde*.

10. Against Bultmann (*John*, 370, 383), who argues that in John 10:11 the phrase means "to stake one's life, risk it, be prepared to lay it down," but that in 10:17–18 it means "to lay down one's life"; so also Bruce, *Gospel of John*, 226. For the meaning "to give oneself up to death," see Barrett, *John*, 374–75; Lindars, *John*, 361; Brown, *John* 1:387; Haenchen, *John*, 2:48; and Schnackenburg, *John* 2:295–96.

11. Barrett, *John*, 375.

12. As Schnackenburg (*John* 2:296) points out, the statements in 11:50–52 make it impossible to interpret *hyper* as referring to a representative death.

13. Brown, *John* 1:399, 504–5.

14. Who the "other sheep" are is a matter of some dispute. I tend to agree with the traditional view that they are Gentiles; so Barrett, *John*, 376; Haenchen, *John* 2:49; Hoskyns, *The Fourth Gospel*, 378; Lindars, *John*, 363; and Schnackenburg, *John* 2:299–300; likewise Bultmann, *John*, 383–84; and Becker, *Evangelium* 1:332—although they assign the passage to the redactor. Martyn (*The Gospel of John in Christian History*, 115–20) argues that they are other Jewish Christians who belong to conventicles known to but separate from the evangelist's community; see also Brown, *The Community of the Beloved Disciple*, 90; idem, "Other Sheep Not of This Fold," *JBL* 97 (1978): 5–22. Finally, Paul Minear ("Audience of the Fourth Evangelist," 257) thinks that these "other sheep" are the "disciples at second hand," i.e. the second generation of believers.

15. Brown, *John* 1:399; and Schnackenburg, *John* 2:300.

16. Schnackenburg, *John* 2:295.

17. Lindars, *John* 427; similarly Schnackenburg, *John* 2:386; and Brown, *John* 1:470, 517. For them the hour is the hour of return to the Father, accomplished through crucifixion, resurrection, and ascension.

18. Nicholson (*Death as Departure*, 145–48) denies that the "hour" is the hour of Jesus' death; rather, it is the hour of his return to the Father and of his glorification. He reaches this conclusion at least partly because he assumes that "the *key* use of the word *hora* occurs in 13:1" (p. 147). Even if this were true, one could simply ignore the uses of "hour" in the Gospel which have in view Jesus' death.

19. The dual character of Jesus' hour is seen again in 13:1. Although the verse explicitly states that the hour is the time of Jesus' departure from the world to his Father and does not explicitly mention Jesus' death or crucifixion, the reference to his imminent betrayal at the hand of Judas Iscariot (13:2) surely brings his death into view; see also Schnackenburg, *John* 2:386.

20. The punctuation of the RSV, which places question marks after

12:27b and 12:27c ("And what shall I say? 'Father, save me from this hour'?") is likely correct. Thus Jesus does not actually pray for deliverance from the hour. One could argue that the Synoptic account, in which Jesus prays that the cup be removed from him but immediately adds, "Nevertheless, thy will be done," does not present a different interpretation of the events. In both instances Jesus recognizes that while death could be avoided, the cross before him represents the Father's will, and for this reason he accepts it (cp. John 18:11). See also Brown's discussion (*John* 1:475–576) of the parallels between John and the Synoptics.

21. Hoskyns, *Fourth Gospel*, 425.

22. Brown suggests three possibilities for interpreting the past and future tenses of the verb "glorify": they may refer to (1) the pre-existent versus the post-resurrectional glory of Jesus; (2) the miracles that Jesus had worked during his ministry (2:11; 11:4, 40) versus the glorification that will occur through the death, resurrection, and ascension; or (3) the entire ministry of Jesus, including the hour, versus the exaltation of Christ, by which he will "draw all men to himself" (12:32). Brown chooses the third option; see *John* 1:476–577. See also Lindars, *John*, 432; and Schnackenburg, *John* 2:388. So also Thüsing (*Die Erhöhung und Verherrlichung Jesu im Johannesevangelium*, 193–98), who points out the parallel to Jesus' statements at John 17:4–5, which likewise look backward and forward: "I glorified thee on earth, having accomplished the work which thou gavest me to do," and "Father, glorify thou me in thy own presence." But in context the passage follows the raising of Lazarus and precedes the passion and hence more likely refers to the glorification through Jesus' signs and death. Becker (*Evangelium* 2:389) captures the gist of the statement in his translation "I glorify it continuously" or "without interruption"; i.e. as the Father has glorified his name in the past, he will continue to do so in the future.

23. Caird, "The Glory of God in the Fourth Gospel: An Exercise in Biblical Semantics," *NTS* 15 (1969): 270.

24. "We can include all references to the hour of his passion as being allusions also to the hour of his glorification. The hour of the passion and death is in a unique sense the hour of his glorification because in it Jesus leaves the world and returns to the Father" (Käsemann, *Testament*, 19). Cp. Nicholson, *Death as Departure*, 145–47.

25. Hoskyns and Davey, *Crucifixion—Resurrection*, 145.

26. Nicholson, *Death as Departure*, 141, 143.

27. For the view that the "fruit" refers to the gentile (or universal) mission, see Barrett, *John*, 422–23; Becker, *Evangelium* 2:383; Brown, *John* 1:470–71; Hoskyns, *Fourth Gospel*, 424; Lindars, *John*, 429; and Schnackenburg, *John* 2:383.

28. At least ten of the references to Jesus as the Son of man allude to

Jesus' death and ascent (3:13–14; 6:27, 53, 62; 8:28; 12:23, 28 [2x]; 13:31.) Moreover, the references to the Son of man in the passion narrative (12:23, 28; 13:31) make specific reference to Jesus' glorification. That Jesus is the Son of man is, for the fourth evangelist, peculiarly linked to his death and glorification by God. See Barrett, *John*, 72; and Caird, "Glory of God," NTS 15 (1969): 269–72.

29. Käsemann, *Testament*, 61.

30. Lindars, *John*, 447; and Haenchen, *John* 2:105; contrast Käsemann, *Letzter Wille*, 49.

31. Brown, *John* 2:563; and Dunn, "The Washing of the Disciples' Feet in John 13:1–20," ZNW 61 (1970): 248.

32. See also Brown, *John* 2:564.

33. See Haenchen, *John* 2:106.

34. Schnackenburg, *John* 3:16; and Becker, *Evangelium* 2:421.

35. Against Bultmann (*John*, 467–68), who argues that it is only knowledge about the event that is referred to the future.

36. Although this is in the first place a reference to the betrayal, as the scriptural citation makes plain, it implies Jesus' death as well, for it is the betrayal which leads to his arrest and subsequent condemnation.

37. On the "I am" statements without predicates, cp. Barrett, *John*, 342; and Brown, *John* 1:533–38.

38. As the commentaries point out, *eis telos* may be taken as meaning either "utterly, completely" or "to the end." Barrett (*John*, 438) comments that it would be characteristic of John for the phrase to mean both things.

39. Barrett (*John*, 440) points out that the degrading character of this task should not be exaggerated, for disciples often washed the feet of their rabbis ("teachers").

40. Barrett (*John*, 441) notes the similarity between Peter's remarks in John and in Mark 8:33; in both instances, Peter is in danger of taking the wrong side with respect to the necessity of Jesus' death.

41. Brown, *John* 2:566; and Schnackenburg, *John* 3:19.

42. This interpretation is based on the shorter reading of John 13:10 ("He who has bathed does not need to wash, but he is clean all over"); so also Barrett, *John*, 441; Brown, *John* 2:568; Bultmann, *John*, 469; Dunn, "Washing of the Disciples' Feet," ZNW 61 (1970): 250–51; Hoskyns, *Fourth Gospel*, 439; Lindars, *John*, 451; Schnackenburg, *John* 3:20–22; and Thyen, "Johannes 13," 348. The longer reading assigns to the footwashing only secondary importance, something necessary even after a complete bath. But in light of v. 8b, such an interpretation of Jesus' act seems precluded, for the footwashing is no trivial additional washing but itself the complete bath. Evidently, then, the evangelist uses "bathe" and "wash" synonymously.

43. In 8:31–36, Jesus promises those who "abide in my word" that they

will be his disciples and be free, rather than remaining as "slaves to sin." The thought is similar to that in 13:10 and 15:3 even though the words and images are different.

44. Culpepper (*Anatomy*, 95) comments that Peter's faithlessness (i.e., his denial) discloses that "whatever Jesus accomplished with his disciples during his ministry, it was not enough. The necessity of Jesus' death is established by the disciples' faithlessness." Culpepper's remark seems to support the interpretation of "clean" suggested here, namely, that "cleanness" is intimately linked to being a faithful disciple and that it is secured only through Jesus' death.

45. See e.g. Richter, "Die Deutung des Kreuzestodes Jesu," in *Studien zum Johannesevangelium*, 58–73; and Thyen, "Johannes 13," 343–56; and the criticism by Dunn in "Washing of the Disciples' Feet," *ZNW* 61 (1970) 249.

46. Becker, *Evangelium* 2:419.

47. Brown, *John* 2:569.

48. Bultmann, *John*, 475; cp. Thyen, "Niemand hat grössere Liebe," 479ff.

49. See Barrett, *John* 440.

50. Thus Bultmann's formulation that Jesus' death disclosed nothing more than did the incarnation itself is unacceptable.

51. Moreover, although Käsemann purports to deal only with chap. 17, he makes assertions about the Gospel that go far beyond that chap. The subtitle of the translated version of *Letzter Wille*—"A Study of the Gospel of John in Light of Chapter 17"—aptly summarizes the book.

52. See Käsemann, *Letzter Wille*, 148.

53. Käsemann, *Testament*, 7.

54. Beutler, "Die Heilsbedeutung des Todes Jesu im Johannesevangelium nach Joh 13,1–20." Similarly, both Müller ("Die Bedeutung des Kreuzestodes im Johannesevangelium," *KD* 21 [1975]: 69) and Käsemann (*Letzter Wille*, 39) argue that John's interpretation of Jesus' death has a spiritual kinship with the *theologia gloriae* preached by the enthusiast— and possibly gnosticizing—opponents of Paul at Corinth.

55. Richardson ("Introduction to the Letters of Ignatius," in *Early Christian Fathers*, 75, 79) speaks of Ignatius' "impatience" and "exaggerated passion" for martyrdom. This attitude certainly goes far beyond the submission and voluntary nature of Jesus' death as portrayed in John's Gospel.

56. See Haenchen, *John* 2:181; and Bultmann, *John*, 659.

57. Meeks, *Prophet-King*, 70; cp. Dodd, *Interpretation*, 473; and Moloney, *The Johannine Son of Man*, 205–7.

58. Culpepper, *Anatomy*, 171; see also Sidebottom, *The Christ of the Fourth Gospel*, 96; Smalley, *John: Evangelist and Interpreter*, 195–96; and Duke, *Irony*, 105–7.

59. Morris (*The Gospel according to John*, 793) suggests the expression could be taken, "Here is the accused."

60. This is pointed out in many ways by various authors. See Bruce, *Gospel of John*, 359; Duke, *Irony*, 106–7; MacRae, "Theology and Irony in the Fourth Gospel," 92; and Sevenster, "Remarks on the Humanity of Jesus in the Gospel and Letters of John," 187.

61. Sevenster, "Remarks on the Humanity of Jesus," 186–87.

62. Bultmann, *John*, 659.

63. Schnackenburg's formulation (*John* 3:284) that John wanted to "replace the synoptic saying about Jesus having been forsaken by God" is less than felicitous.

64. That the saying refers to both the end of Jesus' life and the completion of his work is possible in view of the Johannine fondness for double meanings (so Morris, *John*, 815 n. 73; and Barrett, *John*, 554).

65. Brown, *John* 2:931; and Schnackenburg, *John* 3:284.

66. Against Barrett (*John*, 556), who states that "if Jesus was already dead . . . there was no motive for the lance thrust, unless we are to suppose that the soldier struck Jesus out of mere spite or casual cruelty." But in the context of the narrative, the soldier wishes to be sure of Jesus' death; so, among others, Bruce, *Gospel of John*, 375; Lindars, *John*, 586; Morris, *John*, 818; and Schnackenburg, *John* 3:289.

67. See Barrett, *John*, 556; Brown, *John* 2:947; Bruce, *Gospel of John*, 375–76; and Schnackenburg, *John* 3:289. Haenchen's remark (*John* 2:195) that "since the circulation of the blood had ceased in someone who was already dead, the event is conceivable only as a miracle" is anachronistic. Of course, it is still possible that the Gospel viewed the occurrence as miraculous (Bultmann, *John*, 677).

68. Brown, *John* 2:947.

69. Against Becker, *Evangelium* 2:599–600; and Bultmann, *John*, 677.

70. See the discussion in Brown's *John* 2:946–52.

71. Barrett, *John*, 557.

72. See Dunn, *Unity and Diversity in the New Testament*, 301–2; Meeks, review of Käsemann's *Testament, USQR* 24 (1969): 419; Wengst, *Bedrängte Gemeinde*, 110; Smalley, *John: Evangelist and Interpreter*, 224; Fortna, "Christology in the Fourth Gospel: Redaction-Critical Perspectives," *NTS* 21 (1974–75): 497; Becker, *Evangelium* 2:402–3; and Bornkamm, "Towards the Interpretation of John's Gospel," 89.

73. Meeks, review of Käsemann's *Testament, USQR* 24 (1969): 419.

74. This charge can be leveled against Käsemann; it is particularly true of Müller's study "Die Bedeutung des Kreuzestodes im Johannesevangelium."

75. Nicholson, *Death as Departure*, 163.

76. See Haenchen, "History and Interpretation in the Johannine Passion Narrative," *Int* 24 (1970): 198–219.

77. Ibid., 219.

78. See Bornkamm, "Towards the Interpretation of John's Gospel," 87–89; Hoskyns and Davey, *Crucifixion—Resurrection*, 137–38, 141, 145, 159–62; and Culpepper, *Anatomy*, 22–34.

79. Culpepper, *Anatomy*, 28.

80. Hoskyns and Davey, *Crucifixion—Resurrection*, 152; see also Bornkamm, "Towards the Interpretation of John's Gospel," 89; Culpepper, *Anatomy*, 28, 30; and Forestell, *Word of the Cross*, 64.

EPILOGUE: THE HUMANITY OF JESUS IN THE PERSPECTIVE OF THE FOURTH GOSPEL

1. Bultmann, *John*, 63; cp. Wengst, *Bedrängte Gemeinde*, 118.

2. Culpepper, *Anatomy*, 109.

3. Unlike the gnostic *Apocalypse of Peter* 81:5–24, in which the "living Jesus" laughs at his persecutors while they crucify his "fleshly part," the Gospel of John portrays Jesus' death as an occasion of very real sorrow which only later turns to joy (16:6, 22–24) and only later is understood as Jesus' overcoming of the world (14:29; 16:33).

4. So also Becker, "Aus der Literatur (1978–80)," *ThR* 47 (1982): 312.

5. Nicol, *The Semeia in the Fourth Gospel*, 135.

6. Smith, "The Presentation of Jesus in the Fourth Gospel," 286.

7. De Jonge, *Jesus: Stranger from Heaven*, 98.

8. Culpepper, *Anatomy*, 27–34.

9. Whitacre, *Johannine Polemic*, 68.

10. Sykes, "The Theology of the Humanity of Christ," 66.

BIBLIOGRAPHY

Ashton, John, ed. *The Interpretation of John.* Philadelphia: Fortress Press; London: SPCK, 1986.

Bammel, Ernst. " 'John Did No Miracle.' " In *Miracles: Cambridge Studies in Their Philosophy and History,* ed. C. F. D. Moule, 181–202. Oxford: A. R. Mowbray, 1965.

Barrett, C. K. *Essays on John.* Philadelphia: Westminster Press; London: SPCK, 1982.

————. " 'The Father Is Greater Than I' (Jo 14:28): Subordinationist Christology in the New Testament." In *Neues Testament und Kirche: Für Rudolf Schnackenburg,* ed. J. Gnilka, 144–59. Freiburg: Herder & Herder, 1974.

————. *The Gospel according to St. John.* 2d ed. Philadelphia: Westminster Press, 1978.

————. "The Prologue of St. John's Gospel." In *New Testament Essays,* 27–48. London: SPCK, 1972.

Baur, F. C. *Kritische Untersuchungen über die kanonischen Evangelien, ihr Verhältnis zu einander, ihren Charakter und Ursprung.* Tübingen: Fues, 1847.

————. *Vorlesungen über neutestamentliche Theologie.* 1865. Darmstadt: Wissenschaftliche Buchgesellschaft, 1973.

Becker, Jürgen. "Aus der Literatur zum Johannesevangelium (1978–80)." *ThR* 47 (1982): 279–301, 305–47.

————. "Beobachtungen zum Dualismus im Johannesevangelium." *ZNW* 65 (1974): 71–87.

————. *Das Evangelium nach Johannes.* 2 vols. Gütersloh: Gerd Mohn; Würzburg: Echter-Verlag, 1979–81.

————. "Wunder und Christologie: Zum literarkritischen und christologischen Problem der Wunder im Johannesevangelium." *NTS* 16 (1970): 130–48.

Bernard, J. H. *A Critical and Exegetical Commentary on the Gospel according to St. John.* 2 vols. ICC. Edinburgh: T. & T. Clark, 1928.

Beutler, Johannes. "Die Heilsbedeutung des Todes Jesu im Johannesevangelium nach Joh 13,1–20." In *Der Tod Jesus,* ed. K. Kertelge, 188–204. QD 74. Freiburg: Herder & Herder, 1976.

Borgen, Peder. *Bread from Heaven: An Exegetical Study in the Concept of Manna in the Gospel of John and the Writings of Philo.* NovTSup 10. Leiden: E. J. Brill, 1965.

Bornkamm, Günther. "Die eucharistische Rede im Johannes-Evangelium." *ZNW* 47 (1956): 161–169.

———. "Towards the Interpretation of John's Gospel: A Discussion of *The Testament of Jesus* by Ernst Käsemann (1968)." In *The Interpretation of John,* ed. J. Ashton, 79–98. Philadelphia: Fortress Press, 1986.

———. "Vorjohanneische Tradition oder nachjohanneische Bearbeitung in der eucharistischen Rede Johannes 6?" In *Geschichte und Glaube,* 2:51–64. Gesammelte Aufsätze vol. 4. BEvT 53. Munich: Chr. Kaiser Verlag, 1971.

Brown, Raymond E. *The Community of the Beloved Disciple.* New York: Paulist Press, 1979.

———. "Does the New Testament Call Jesus God?" In *Jesus: God and Man,* 1–38. Milwaukee: Bruce Publishing, 1967.

———. *The Gospel according to John.* 2 vols. Anchor Bible. Garden City, N.Y.: Doubleday & Co., 1966–70.

———. "Other Sheep Not of This Fold: The Johannine Perspective on Christian Diversity in the Late First Century." *JBL* 97 (1978): 5–22.

———. "The Problem of Historicity in John." In *New Testament Essays.* 143–67. New York: Paulist Press, 1965.

Bruce, F. F. *The Gospel of John: Introduction, Exposition, and Notes.* Grand Rapids: Wm. B. Eerdmans, 1983.

Bultmann, Rudolf. *The Gospel of John: A Commentary.* Trans. G. W. Beasley-Murray. Philadelphia: Westminster Press, 1971.

———. "Der religionsgeschichtliche Hintergrund des Prologs zum Johannes-Evangelium." *Eucharisterion: Studien zur Religion des Alten und Neuen Testaments—Für Hermann Gunkel,* ed. Hans Schmidt, 2:3–26. Göttingen: Vandenhoeck & Ruprecht, 1923.

———. *Theology of the New Testament.* 2 vols. Trans. Kendrick Grobel. New York: Charles Scribner's Sons, 1951–55.

Caird, G. B. "The Glory of God in the Fourth Gospel: An Exercise in Biblical Semantics." *NTS* 15 (1969): 265–77.

Charlesworth, J. H. "The Concept of the Messiah in the Pseudepigrapha." In *ANRW* 19/1, ed. Wolfgang Haase, 188–218. Berlin: Walter de Gruyter, 1979.

————, ed. *The Old Testament Pseudepigrapha*. 2 vols. New York: Doubleday & Co., 1983–85.

Corley, Bruce, ed. *Colloquy on New Testament Studies: A Time for Reappraisal and Fresh Approaches*. Macon, Ga.: Mercer Univ. Press, 1983.

Culpepper, R. Alan. *Anatomy of the Fourth Gospel: A Study in Literary Design*. Philadelphia: Fortress Press, 1983.

Davies, W. D. *The Gospel and the Land: Early Christianity and Jewish Territorial Doctrine*. Berkeley and Los Angeles: Univ. of California Press, 1974.

De Jonge, Marinus. *Jesus—Stranger from Heaven and Son of God: Jesus Christ and the Christians in Johannine Perspective*, ed. and trans. John E. Steely. Missoula, Mont.: Scholars Press, 1977.

Demke, Christoph. "Der sogenannte Logos-Hymnus im johanneischen Prolog." *ZNW* 58 (1967): 45–68.

Dodd, C. H. *Historical Tradition in the Fourth Gospel*. Cambridge: Cambridge Univ. Press, 1963.

————. *The Interpretation of the Fourth Gospel*. Cambridge: Cambridge Univ. Press, 1953.

Duke, Paul D. *Irony in the Fourth Gospel*. Richmond: John Knox Press, 1985.

Dunn, James D. G. "John 6: A Eucharistic Discourse?" *NTS* 17 (1971): 328–38.

————. *Unity and Diversity in the New Testament*. Philadelphia: Westminster Press, 1977.

————. "The Washing of the Disciples' Feet in John 13:1–20." *ZNW* 61 (1970): 247–52.

Fennema, David. "Jesus and God according to John: An Analysis of the Fourth Gospel's Father/Son Christology." Ph.D. diss., Duke University, 1979.

————. "John 1:18: 'God the Only Son.'" *NTS* 31 (1985): 124–35.

Forestell, J. Terence, C.S.B. *The Word of the Cross: Salvation as Revelation in the Fourth Gospel*. AnBib 57. Rome: Biblical Institute Press, 1974.

Fortna, Robert T. "Christology in the Fourth Gospel: Redaction-Critical Perspectives." *NTS* 21 (1974–75): 489–504.

————. *The Gospel of Signs*. SNTSMS 11. Cambridge: Cambridge Univ. Press, 1970.

————. "Theological Use of Locale in the Fourth Gospel." In *Gospel Studies in Honor of Sherman E. Johnson*, 58–95. *ATR* supp. ser. 3 (March 1974).

Giblin, Charles H. "Suggestion, Negative Response, and Positive Action in St. John's Portrayal of Jesus (John 2.1–11.; 4.46–54.; 7.2–14.; 11.1–44.)." *NTS* 26 (1980): 197–211.

Haenchen, Ernst. *A Commentary on the Gospel of John*. 2 vols. Ed. Robert

W. Funk and Ulrich Busse; trans. Robert W. Funk. Philadelphia: Fortress Press, 1984.

———. *Gott und Mensch*. Tübingen: J. C. B. Mohr (Paul Siebeck), 1965.

———. "History and Interpretation in the Johannine Passion Narrative." *Int* 24 (1970): 198–219.

Hegermann, Harald. "Er kam in sein Eigentum: Zur Bedeutung des Erdenwirkens Jesu im vierten Evangelium." In *Der Ruf Jesu und die Antwort der Gemeinde: Für Joachim Jeremias*, ed. Eduard Lohse, 112–31. Göttingen: Vandenhoeck & Ruprecht, 1970.

Hirsch, Emanuel. *Das vierte Evangelium in seiner ursprünglichen Gestalt verdeutscht und erklärt*. Tübingen: J. C. B. Mohr (Paul Siebeck), 1936.

Hooker, Morna D. "The Johannine Prologue and the Messianic Secret." *NTS* 21 (1974): 40–58.

Hoskyns, Edwyn Clement. *The Fourth Gospel*. 2d rev. ed. Ed. Francis Noel Davey. London: Faber & Faber, 1957.

Hoskyns, Edwyn Clement, and Francis Noel Davey. *Crucifixion—Resurrection: The Pattern of the Theology and Ethics of the New Testament*. London: SPCK, 1981.

Johnson, Luke T. *The Writings of the New Testament: An Interpretation*. Philadelphia: Fortress Press, 1986.

Käsemann, Ernst. *Jesu letzter Wille nach Johannes 17*. 3d ed. Tübingen: J. C. B. Mohr (Paul Siebeck), 1971.

———. "Ketzer und Zeuge: Zum Johanneischen Verfasserproblem." In *Exegetische Versuche und Besinnungen* 1:168–87. Göttingen: Vandenhoeck & Ruprecht, 1960.

———. "The Structure and Purpose of the Prologue to John's Gospel." In *New Testament Questions of Today*, 138–67. Philadelphia: Fortress Press, 1969.

———. *The Testament of Jesus: A Study of the Gospel of John in the Light of Chapter 17*. 2d ed. Trans. Gerhard Krodel. Philadelphia: Fortress Press, 1968.

Klausner, Joseph. *The Messianic Idea in Israel*. New York: Macmillan Co., 1955.

Koester, Helmut. Comment in "Seminar Dialogue with Helmut Koester," in *Colloquy on New Testament Studies: A Time for Reappraisal and Fresh Approaches,* ed. Bruce Corley (Macon, Ga.: Mercer Univ. Press, 1983), 75.

———. "History and Cult in the Gospel of John and in Ignatius of Antioch." In *The Bultmann School of Biblical Interpretation: New Directions?* 111–23. *JTC* 1. New York: Harper & Row; Tübingen: J. C. B. Mohr (Paul Siebeck), 1965.

———. *Introduction to the New Testament*. Vol. 2, *History and Literature of Early Christianity*. Philadelphia: Fortress Press, 1982.

Kysar, Robert. "Christology and Controversy: The Contributions of the Prologue of the Gospel of John to New Testament Christology and Their Historical Setting." *CurTM* 5 (1978): 348–64.

————. *The Fourth Evangelist and His Gospel: An Examination of Contemporary Scholarship.* Minneapolis: Augsburg Pub. House, 1975.

Langbrandtner, Wolfgang. *Weltferner Gott oder Gott der Liebe? Der Ketzerstreit in der johanneischen Kirche.* BEvT 6. Frankfurt am Main: Peter Lang, 1977.

Lattke, Michael. *Einheit im Wort: Die spezifische Bedeutung von agape, agapan und philein im Johannesevangelium.* SANT 41. Munich: Kösel-Verlag, 1975.

Lieu, Judith M. "Gnosticism and the Gospel of John." *ExpTim* 90 (1979): 233–37.

Lindars, Barnabas. *Behind the Fourth Gospel.* London: SPCK, 1971.

————. *The Gospel of John.* New Century Bible. Grand Rapids: Wm. B. Eerdmans, 1972.

Lohse, Eduard. "Wort und Sakrament im Johannesevangelium." *NTS* 7 (1960): 110–25.

MacRae, George, S.J. "Theology and Irony in the Fourth Gospel." In *The Word in the World: Essays in Honor of Frederick L. Moriarty, S.J.*, ed. Richard J. Clifford and George W. MacRae, 83–96. Cambridge, Mass.: Weston College Press, 1973.

Martyn, J. L. *The Gospel of John in Christian History: Essays for Interpreters.* New York: Paulist Press, 1978.

————. *History and Theology in the Fourth Gospel.* 2d ed. Nashville: Abingdon Press, 1979.

Mastin, B. A. "A Neglected Feature of the Christology of the Fourth Gospel." *NTS* 22 (1975): 32–51.

Meeks, Wayne A. "Galilee and Judea in the Fourth Gospel." *JBL* 85 (1966): 159–69.

————. "The Man from Heaven in Johannine Sectarianism," *JBL* 91 (1972): 44–72.

————. *The Prophet-King: Moses Traditions and the Johannine Christology.* NovTSup 14. Leiden: E. J. Brill, 1967.

————. Review of *The Testament of Jesus: A Study of the Gospel in the Light of Chapter 17* by Ernst Käsemann. *USQR* 24 (1968–69): 414–20.

Minear, Paul. "The Audience of the Fourth Evangelist." In *Interpreting the Gospels*, ed. James L. Mays, 247–64. Philadelphia: Fortress Press, 1981.

Moloney, Francis J., S.D.B. *The Johannine Son of Man.* 2d ed. BSR 14. Rome: Libreria Ateneo Salesiano, 1979.

Morris, Leon. *The Gospel according to John.* Grand Rapids: Wm. B. Eerdmans, 1971.

Moule, C. F. D. "The Meaning of 'Life' in the Gospels and Epistles of St. John: A Study in the Story of Lazarus, John 11:1–44." *Theology* 78 (1975): 114–25.

Müller, Ulrich B. "Die Bedeutung des Kreuzestodes im Johannesevangelium: Erwägungen zur Kreuzestheologie im Neuen Testament." *KD* 21 (1975): 49–71.

Mussner, Franz. *The Historical Jesus in the Gospel of St. John.* QD 19. New York: Herder & Herder, 1967.

Nicholson, Godfrey C. *Death as Departure: The Johannine Ascent-Descent Schema.* SBLDS 63. Chico, Calif.: Scholars Press, 1983.

Nicol, W. *The Semeia in the Fourth Gospel: Tradition and Redaction.* NovTSup 32. Leiden: E. J. Brill, 1972.

O'Neill, J. C. "The Silence of Jesus," *NTS* 15 (1969): 153–67.

Pryor, John W. "John 4:44 and the *Patris* of Jesus." *CBQ* 49 (1987): 254–63.

Reim, Günter. "John IV.44—Crux or Clue?" *NTS* 22 (1976): 476–80.

Richardson, Cyril C., ed. and trans. *Early Christian Fathers.* LCC 1. Philadelphia: Westminster Press, 1953.

Richter, Georg. "Die Fleischwerdung im Johannesevangelium." *NovT* 13 (1971): 81–126; 14 (1972): 256–76.

———. *Die Fusswaschung im Johannesevangelium. Geschichte ihrer Deutung.* Ed. O. Kuss. BU 1. Regensburg: Friedrich Pustet, 1967.

———. *Studien zum Johannesevangelium.* Ed. Josef Hainz. BU 13. Regensburg: Friedrich Pustet, 1977.

Ridderbos, Herman. "The Structure and Scope of the Prologue to the Gospel of John." *NovT* 8 (1966): 179–201.

Schenke, Ludger. "Die formale und gedankliche Struktur von Joh 6,26–58." *BZ* 24 (1980): 21–41.

Schnackenburg, Rudolf. *The Gospel according to St. John.* 3 vols. New York: Seabury Press, 1980; New York: Crossroad, 1982.

———. "Logos-Hymnus und johanneischer Prolog." *BZ* 1 (1957): 69–109.

———. "Der Menschensohn im Johannesevangelium." *NTS* 11 (1964–65): 123–37.

———. "Die Messiasfrage im Johannesevangelium." In *Neutestamentliche Aufsätze: Für Josef Schmid,* ed. J. Binzler, O. Kuss, F. Mussner, 240–64. Regensburg: Friedrich Pustet, 1963.

Schneider, Johannes. "Zur Frage der Komposition von Joh. 6:27–58 (59) (*Die Himmelsbrotrede*)." In *In Memoriam Ernst Lohmeyer,* ed. Werner Schmauch, 132–42. Stuttgart: Evangelisches Verlagswerk, 1951.

Schottroff, Luise. *Der Glaubende und die feindliche Welt: Beobachtungen zum gnostischen Dualismus und seiner Bedeutung für Paulus und das Johannesevangelium.* Neukirchen-Vluyn: Neukirchener Verlag, 1970.

Schürmann, Heinz. "Jo 6:51c—Ein Schlüssel zur grossen johanneischen Brotrede." In *Ursprung und Gestalt: Erörterungen und Besinnungen zum Neuen Testament*, 150–66. Düsseldorf: Patmos-Verlag, 1970.

Schweizer, Eduard. "Das johanneische Zeugnis von Herrenmahl." In *Neotestamentica: Deutsche und Englische Aufsätze, 1951–1963*, 384–94. Zurich and Stuttgart: Zwingli Verlag, 1963.

Sevenster, G. "Remarks on the Humanity of Jesus in the Gospel and Letters of John." In *Studies in John: Presented to Professor Dr. J. N. Sevenster on the Occasion of His Seventieth Birthday*, 185–93. NovTSup 24. Leiden: E. J. Brill, 1970.

Sidebottom, E. M. *The Christ of the Fourth Gospel: In the Light of First-Century Thought*. London: SPCK, 1961.

Smalley, Stephen. *John: Evangelist and Interpreter*. Exeter: Paternoster, 1978.

———. " 'The Testament of Jesus': Another Look." In *SE* 6:495–501. Berlin: Akademie-Verlag, 1973.

Smith, D. Moody. *The Composition and Order of the Fourth Gospel: Bultmann's Literary Theory*. New Haven: Yale Univ. Press, 1965.

———. "The Presentation of Jesus in the Fourth Gospel." In *Interpreting the Gospels*, ed. James L. Mays, 278–90. Philadelphia: Fortress Press, 1981.

Sykes, S. W. "The Theology of the Humanity of Christ." In *Christ, Faith, and History: Cambridge Studies in Christology*, ed. S. W. Sykes and J. P. Clayton, 53–71. Cambridge: Cambridge Univ. Press, 1972.

Taylor, Vincent. "Does the New Testament Call Jesus God?" In *New Testament Essays*, 83–89. London: Epworth Press, 1970.

Theissen, Gerd. *The Miracle Stories of the Early Christian Tradition*. Ed. John Riches; trans. Francis McDonagh. Edinburgh: T. & T. Clark, 1983.

Thompson, Marianne Meye. "The Humanity of Jesus in the Gospel of John." Ph.D. diss., Duke Univ., 1985.

Thüsing, Wilhelm. *Die Erhöhung und Verherrlichung Jesu im Johannesevangelium*. 3d ed. NTAbh 21/1, 2. Münster: Aschendorff, 1979.

Thyen, Hartwig. "Aus der Literatur zum Johannesevangelium." *ThR* 39 (1974): 1–69, 221–52, 289–330; 42 (1977): 211–70; 43 (1978): 328–59; 44 (1979): 97–134.

———. " 'Denn wir lieben die Brüder' (1 Joh 3,14)." In *Rechtfertigung: Für Ernst Käsemann*, ed. Johannes Friedrich, Wolfgang Pohlmann, Peter Stuhlmacher, 527–42. Tübingen: J. C. B. Mohr (Paul Siebeck); Göttingen: Vandenhoeck & Ruprecht, 1976.

———. "Entwicklungen innerhalb der johanneischen Theologie und Kirche im Spiegel von Joh 21 und der Lieblingsjüngertexte des Evangeliums." In *L'Evangile de Jean: Sources, rédaction, théologie*, ed. M. de Jonge, 259–99. Louvain: University Press, 1977.

————. "Johannes 13 und die 'kirchliche Redaktion' des vierten Evangeliums." In *Tradition und Glaube: Das frühe Christentum in seiner Umwelt—Festgabe für Karl Georg Kuhn*, ed. Gert Jeremias, Heinz-Wolfgang Kuhn, Hartmut Stegemann, 343–56. Göttingen: Vandenhoeck & Ruprecht, 1971.

————. " 'Niemand hat grössere Liebe als die, dass er sein Leben für seine Freunde hingibt' (Joh 15,13): Das johanneische Verständnis des Kreuzestodes Jesus." In *Theologia Crucis—Signum Crucis: Festschrift für Erich Dinkler*, ed. Carl Andresen and Gunter Klein, 467–81. Tübingen: J. C. B. Mohr (Paul Siebeck), 1979.

Wengst, Klaus. *Bedrängte Gemeinde und verherrlichter Christus: Der historische Ort des Johannesevangeliums als Schlüssel zur seiner Interpretation.* Neukirchen-Vluyn: Neukirchener Verlag, 1981.

Wetter, G. P. *"Der Sohn Gottes": Eine Untersuchung über die Charakter und die Tendenz des Johannes-Evangeliums.* Göttingen: Vandenhoeck & Ruprecht, 1916.

Whitacre, Rodney A. *Johannine Polemic: The Role of Tradition and Theology.* SBLDS 67. Chico, Calif.: Scholars Press, 1982.

Wilckens, Ulrich. "Der eucharistische Abschnitt der johanneischen Rede vom Lebensbrot (Joh 6:51c–58)." In *Neues Testament und Kirche: Festschrift für Rudolf Schnackenburg*, ed. J. Gnilka, 220–48. Freiburg: Herder & Herder, 1974.

Wilkens, Wilhelm. *Zeichen und Werke: Ein Beitrag zur Theologie des 4. Evangeliums in Erzählungs- und Redestoff.* Zurich: Zwingli Verlag, 1969.

Windisch, Hans. "Der johanneische Erzählungsstil." In *Eucharisterion: Studien zur Religion und Literatur des Alten und Neuen Testaments—Festschrift für Hermann Gunkel*, ed. Hans Schmidt, 2:174–213. Göttingen: Vandenhoeck & Ruprecht, 1923.

Wrede, D. W. *Charakter und Tendenz des Johannesevangeliums.* Tübingen: J. C. B. Mohr (Paul Siebeck), 1933.

AUTHOR INDEX

SCRIPTURE INDEX

165